HARD STOP

A LIFE OF VIOLENCE, CRIME AND DECEPTION

JACK DAWE

Copyright © 2022 Jack Dawe

The moral right of the author has been asserted.

Apart from any fair dealing for the purposes of research or private study, or criticism or review, as permitted under the Copyright, Designs and Patents Act 1988, this publication may only be reproduced, stored or transmitted, in any form or by any means, with the prior permission in writing of the publishers, or in the case of reprographic reproduction in accordance with the terms of licences issued by the Copyright Licensing Agency. Enquiries concerning reproduction outside those terms should be sent to the publishers.

Matador
Unit E2 Airfield Business Park,
Harrison Road, Market Harborough,
Leicestershire. LE16 7UL
Tel: 0116 2792299
Email: books@troubador.co.uk
Web: www.troubador.co.uk/matador
Twitter: @matadorbooks

ISBN 978 1803131 856

British Library Cataloguing in Publication Data.
A catalogue record for this book is available from the British Library.

Printed and bound in Great Britain by CMP UK
Typeset in 11pt Minion Pro by Troubador Publishing Ltd, Leicester, UK

Matador is an imprint of Troubador Publishing Ltd

DEDICATIONS AND ACKNOWLEDGMENTS

Owen & Mollie, ma Raison d'être
My Parents for building my strong foundations
Friends and loved ones who have helped me write this book,
especially Hayley who corrected my poor grammar and spelling.
Those inappropriate role models who never abandoned me
The brave members of the Military who I have served alongside
The unsung heroes of the thin blue line who risk their lives daily
Front cover photo by Ian BROWN.

AUTHORS NOTE

My story is not an expose of police corruption and tactics, nor is it a chance to talk bad about people and try and score points off of others misfortune. I have changed some names, mine included, mostly to protect the guilty, but also for the anonymity of those who choose to live the quiet life. I have changed some locations and I have omitted details of tactics and equipment that the Police use in the covert fight against crime, some may comment that I shouldn't even tell my story. However, I do believe that what I am disclosing is already in the public arena on countless TV shows and of no risk to modern day operatives.

Throughout this book I am telling the truth, as I recall it,

It is about things that happened to me during my life, I do not apologise for the stupid actions of a young man who grew up in circumstances that many have never experienced, I can state though, that like most young people, I learnt from my mistakes and moved forward with my life.

I do not profess to be a special forces soldier or a tough guy, and I do not claim to be the best cop that ever served in the Police, what I was though, was a determined young man who had a thirst for adventure and the willingness to take risks.

The Police are on the frontline of the fight against crime every day, how many jobs do you know where you are put in harm's way every time you go to work? Police Officers are never off duty and are held to a higher standard in society, this severely impacts on their social lives, they are always under the scrutiny of people who have no idea what the world is really like outside of their comfortable world of social media judgements. The public want the Police to destroy the monsters, but they don't want to witness how it is done, nor do they want to experience the violence and intrusion on people's freedoms that often goes with the territory. As a result of this lack of grit from some quarters we have lost the streets to Drug Dealers and Knife wielding kids who have never been Policed with robust tactics, I don't mean the lies you have been told about the old beat officer giving kids a clip around the ear for stealing apples, I'm talking about fighting violence with violence. Criminals and Police Officers will die, so, future Politicians, Soldiers and Police Officers take note, if you don't have the stomach for a true war where people die and get injured, then you have no business being on the battlefield!

"We sleep soundly in our beds because rough men stand ready in the night to visit violence on those who would do us harm."
(Winston Churchill)

PROLOGUE

LEICESTER V LEEDS 24th October 2017

We moved upwards into the heights of the football stadium in an attempt to dissect the 'Hard Core' football fans and hold this crowd back from their position of advantage. The crowd surged forward towards us again and threw the weight of their bodies down the stands into us like a crashing wave. This wave of bodies impacted into me throwing me into the sterile seating area that is supposed to act as a buffer zone between opposing football supporters. The fibrous rip I felt in my lower back shot through my body like an electric shock from the base of my spine to the tips of my extremities. I was disorientated, dazed, and fighting my bodies urge to drop to the floor and scream. All I could feel was the constant stabbing pain and weakness in my lower back and limbs and the adrenaline began to course through me, this was not a time to curl up in a ball and surrender, I had to fight through this and maintain our 'thin blue line'! After 90 punishing minutes the match finally concluded 3-1 to Leicester, the fans played out the usual after match shenanigans and eventually we were stood down for the evening. When I arrived home my body stank after so many hours of jostling with people whilst weighed down with my PPE and body armour. I poured myself a stiff drink, lay on the floor and let the damage to my body begin to unwind and reveal how injured I actually was.

HARD STOP

After nearly 3 years of suffering the pain became too much and in April 2020 my mind and body just gave up, I had been on various medications including Morphine since 2017, I also subsidised the medications with alcohol in an attempt to block out the pain. I had become dependent on the crutch of alcohol for many years to cope with the stress of work and home life, but now I was actively using the booze to block out my pain and to help me into an unsettled non-productive sleep. I often drank alone and the booze supressed my inner demons that hated my pain ridden existence, this led to procrastination about stopping the drinking, getting fit again and making some positive moves in my career. These goals were short lived and more than once or twice I woke in the morning still with the taste of drink on my breath, I would also have a stinking headache to accompany my dizzy hangover and drink fuelled anxiety. I often walked to work, I was kidding myself that it was part of my health kick, but in reality it was because I didn't want to risk the career ending prospect of being pulled over by the Police in my car and failing a breathalyser test. I was a ticking time bomb of physical pain and associated mental anguish, I genuinely considered that if I was to live in this pain for the rest of my life I would have ended it on my own terms, I had even planned how I would have done it. I knew these were danger signs and that I was in a dark place, I only hoped I was able to get the help I needed. However, the world was in lockdown due to the COVID-19 epidemic and the NHS were unable to help me, they had more pressing concerns so just kept supplying me with as much medication as I wanted. MRI scans were done and the surgeon diagnosed me with prolapsed discs in my lower lumber area, the disks were smashing into my central nervous system, which in turn caused the disabling pain in my leg. This diagnosis led to spinal surgery at a private clinic, again the NHS were unable to help, this reduced the pain significantly and allowed me to live a less painful existence.

PROLOGUE

What followed next was a stomach cramping, sleepless journey, like that of a recovering heroin addict; The 'Rattle' of my withdrawals from the morphine I had been prescribed and the constant grind of pain bought out vivid memories of a life of violence, crime and deception that spanned over 30 years of active service as a Soldier and a front-line Police Officer. These memories had been locked away and hidden to protect me from reliving them every day, at times though, in a drug induced haze, memories once forgotten both good and bad came charging forward into vivid memory,

I have therefore decided to tell my story.

YARDIES

(A Yardie is a member of a secret criminal organization based in Jamaica, which is especially associated with drug dealing and extreme violence.)

I saw the twists of the rifling in the barrel that protruded from the smooth top slide of the black 9mm Berretta pistol that was pointing directly at my face! The pistol was well used and had a patina of wear and tear you associated with a craftsman's tools; with areas of light bare metal where it has been slid in and out of a holster a 1000 times and light scratches from the day to day use you would expect of an Authorised Firearms Officer (AFO)!

The AFO wore old worn blue jeans and a large black hooded tactical coat under which he was wearing black body armour, on his head he wore the black baseball cap of an armed Police Officer. The cap had the black and white chequered band on the sides and the words Police across the front. The cap was greying and well-worn, the sign of an experienced operator who had worn the same cap day in and day out for years in all weather conditions. He was too far away for me to make a grab for his weapon, but close enough to deliver a double tap of 9mm parabellum into the centre of my chest if he saw me as a threat. He stood with his feet spread in a fighter stance, his left foot pointing forward and his right foot planted to the rear and out at an angle, his legs were slightly bent at the knees with his left shoulder pointed forward which bladed his body to the side to not present a large target. His arms were punched out front pushing the weapon forward with a slight bend in his left arm forming a stable but reactive platform. His eyes peered down the barrel with an emotionless focus ensuring the point of the front sight sat in between the gap of the rear sight, this would deliver a well-aimed shot from the pistol that would hit its target.

My hands were outstretched to the sky showing that they were empty, and I had no weapons in the palms of my hands, this was the classic 'I surrender' pose. I was now under his control and remained in a submissive stance as I was ordered to the floor.

"POLICE!!! Hands, show me your hands, down to the floor" he barked!

I began to crouch to the tarmac floor and fully complied with his orders, this guy couldn't 100% be sure we were the undercover officers involved in this operation. We may have moved on and some real drug addicts or gang members may have walked into the middle of this ambush, they may have been armed or so scared that they would panic and attack the AFO in a fight or flight reaction!

The Italian made Beretta 92f delivered up to 15 rounds of 9mm ammunition from one magazine and I'm sure he was carrying at least another 3. This semi-automatic pistol had been used across the Military and Police for a number of years now and had been proven as a deadly and reliable weapon.

It was a surreal experience to have a loaded gun pointed at me, I was pensive, but I was confident that the experienced cop with the worn out baseball cap had the professionalism not to shoot me, I wasn't going to give him any reason too either, just a squeeze of the trigger and I would be dead. As I continued to crouch down towards the pavement I maintained eye contact with him, I needed to see his eyes and read the expression on his face, he was focused and calm, this was a good combination and a sign I was in safe hands. Just to make sure I decided to give him a cheeky little wink! I saw a twitch of acknowledgement in his eyes, it was a pulse of both eyes, like a half blink, I saw his shoulders relax, this I knew was a sign of relief, he now knew I was one of the good guys and he wasn't going to have to kill someone today!

Moments before we had been swarmed by armed Police Jim and I had been buying our second deal of 'Crack' from DANTE that day. DANTE was a known 'Yardy' from one of the notorious Birmingham Gangs that ran the drug distribution in the city.

DANTE was a Jamaican lad about 25years old, he had light brown skin and short cropped afro hair, he was a fit guy, lean and muscular and looked like he could handle himself if he needed to. He wore black jeans and a tight black t-shirt most of the time and had the obligatory bling with a thick gold kerb chain around his neck and another oversized gold chain on his left wrist. He always had nice cars and never had a shortage of gear to sell, he would drag a sandwich bag of wraps out and pick through them like a Woolworths pick n mix before tossing the deal onto the passenger seat for us to pick up.

You had two distinct Urban Street Gangs in Birmingham, 'The Johnsons' and the 'Burger Bar Crew'. These gangsters were known to be armed and had a tendency for extreme violence. They had only just recently been involved in a revenge shooting where on January the 2nd 2003 two girls Charlene ELLIS aged 18 and Letisha SHAKESPEARE aged 17 were caught in a revenge shooting after the murder of a Burger Bar Yardy! Both had been at a party at a hair salon in the Aston area of the city when they were hit with a flurry of bullets from a MAC-10 machine pistol! This cold blooded and indiscriminate use of violence had sent shock waves across the country and every effort was being made to combat the rising threat of armed Urban Street Gangs, In the West Midlands this meant that 'The Burger bar Crew and Johnsons' were the top priority!

I was fully aware that I was not alone in this scenario, this was the culmination of two months of undercover drugs purchases by myself and Jim in the North Birmingham area. This was a 'Buy & Bust' where we lured our target into an ambush, our intention was to make a drugs purchase during which a firearms team were to carry out a 'Hard stop' arrest and detain the dealer. This extreme tactical use of Firearms Officers was a necessity, we had intelligence that linked DANTE to firearms, and we had no other way of finding out who he actually was or where he lived.

We had begun the day with our own individual briefing about the day's events by the operational team Detective Sergeant (DS), he read us our deployment rules and we began our notebooks for the day in which we recorded the serial numbers of all the money that we had been issued to buy drugs with, the money we spent could have then been compared to the notes found in the possession of the dealer when they were arrested. The Detective Inspector (DI) had had to go to another location to brief the firearms and surveillance teams on the plan, he was armed with footage of us in our street clothes so they had an idea of who we were when the plan was executed!

Soon after the briefing we were dropped into the Wylde Green area of the city by our cover team to make our way to the ambush location where we had, much to the disgust of the residents, bought drugs from DANTE and other dealers on a number of occasions. The chosen road was a small residential road, lined with well-kept semi-detached houses where families and retired people lived. You could see that this was a nice street where the residents cared for their homes and hated our presence, one old guy used to come out and stare at us and tell us to 'Bugger off' whilst we waited for our dealer, this did make me feel guilty but also made me smile that he would never know we were actually cops. We only used the road as it was a road where DANTE had told us to meet him on numerous occasions, you would only go there if you lived there, but it was perfect for our requirements too! The road was off the main drag into town and could easily be blocked and contained as a crime scene without causing a major tail back or too much interest from passers-by. It was also near a phone box so we could put a call in to DANTE when we wanted to get him 'on plot' to buy from him and spring the ambush!

Jim made the call

Ring, Ring, Ring!

We were both crammed into the phone box, it was the old traditional British red type of phone box with a heavy metal door and lots of small glass windows allowing the light in whilst maintaining some privacy. The back wall behind the payphone was plastered with calling cards of different colours for various services from taxi's, massages and ladies of the night! The phone box smelt of a mixture of cigarette smoke, piss and the odours that myself and Jim were adding from our tuna and mud cologne that we wore to keep people away from us.

"**Yo**" answered DANTE

"**Alright mate, its Jim, can you score me a rock, need a teenth, my mate wants one too**" said Jim.

A 'Teenth' is around 1.75 grams, you usually get a better deal if you buy bigger weights! This would cost us about £25 each, which we paid for with the money issued to us during our briefing.

"**We can meet you on the back road again yeah?**" Jim Offered

"**Ya man, be der soon**" came the reply, DANTE was a man of few words, we were just smelly crack heads and he didn't want to be our friend, he wanted our cash and then to get rid of us!

As we waited in the road for DANTE we agreed that Jim would make the deal and drop something to give a bit of a delay so the strike team had enough time to get into the street and block his car. A light blue BMW M3 car pulled into the street from the main Birmingham Road, the dark figure inside was DANTE, he pulled over to us and Jim leaned into the window dropping a handful of change and causing our planned distraction. It was DANTE but he was in a different car than last time, Jim was dragging this out as long as he could, I was looking around frantically panicking that we would miss our opportunity, I knew that we had a surveillance team watching us so I made a pre agreed signal for them to 'STRIKE' and take out the target. DANTE was helping Jim with his loose change so moving slightly away I hoped that my signal was seen by the team and not DANTE, I wanted the strike team to take the hint and come and do their job! Still no team came and we had delayed DANTE as long as we could, where the fuck were they, why hadn't they come? I stormed off to the phone box I was fuming, I rang the DS and asked

"**Where the fuck were you lot, I put the signal in, why didn't you come?**"

His voice was taken aback he was obviously shocked that I challenged him in this way! He began to mumble an answer and finally admitted that the Superintendent in charge had seen a new car and couldn't confirm if it was our target, my signal put him in a tight spot and he bottled it.

"**Right, we are going to phone him back and say we want some more gear and you fuckers are going to take him out … right?**"

There was a muffled pause as he put his hand over the phone and passed a sanitised version of my request to the Superintendent, I heard a discussion going backwards and forwards, he came back with the green light, the Superintendent did have some balls after all, I had to respect that. I hung up the phone receiver and Jim picked it up to call DANTE again, it was no surprise that he agreed to meet us again in 20minutes.

The BMW pulled up to the kerbside and Jim lent in through the open passenger window to talk to DANTE and do the deal. Within seconds I saw cars moving towards us from the right at speed. There were 3 saloon type cars, a mix of Ford Sierras and I think one was a Mondeo, they were low down on their suspensions and I saw large hulking figures silhouetted through the windows. The cars glided towards us as I grabbed the back of Jim's trouser belt and pulled him sharply back out of the passenger window… we staggered backwards to the pavement as the first car was driven into the front offside panel of the BMW, the second stopped blocking the drivers exit and the third drove directly into the rear offside of the car immobilising it by pinning it into a box that it couldn't escape from. The driver's window imploded showering broken glass onto DANTE as it was destroyed by a crowbar and DANTE was hauled out of the driver's seat through the gap where the window once was. Body armour clad AFO's with Beretta pistols and H&K Mp5 rifles swooped from the plain cars securing both myself and Jim by taking us to the ground at gun point. We lay there on the floor with our hands handcuffed behind our backs, I looked around us and saw that the street was now awash with blue lights and uniformed officers blocking the road off, DANTE had 3 armed cops aiming their weapons at him as he lay there also in handcuffs. I was hauled to my feet by two cops and the handcuffs bit into my wrists causing me to yelp in pain, these things do actually hurt!

As I was taken to a waiting Police car I saw the old man who had told us to 'bugger off,' he had his arms crossed and he had a satisfied look on his face that the Police had locked us up, I inwardly chuckled to myself as I was pushed into the rear of the Police Car, he would never know who I actually was or what we had achieved that day.

DANTE tried to say the 2 sandwich bags full of wraps of crack and heroin found in his car belonged to the two lads who were with him when he was arrested, Dante's world fell apart when he was informed that those two lads were undercover Police Officers. DANTE received a 6-year prison sentence in his absence as he fled the country back to the safety of Jamaica.

This was the life of an undercover police officer, it was what I had joined to do, and I loved it!

THIEF

(One who commits the act or crime of theft)

By the age of 14 I had learnt how to kill a man with my bare hands, if I didn't want to get too close I knew how to shoot the same man, with deadly accuracy, up to 300m away with a rifle! I could navigate and survive comfortably in the wilderness, and I was also able to hold my own on a boat at sea if needed. To add to this impressive list of life skills I had acquired, I drank and swore like a Sailor and I had also become a bit of a mini crime wave too! This young introduction into a life of violence and crime had not come about as a result of years of poverty, neglect or abuse by my parents, we weren't even at war… I was a child of the 70's and 80's, it was normal life!

Not only did we have the best music genre ever! We also had freedom to roam and to experience life in a way that seems to be alien to my own children. Very few kids had games consoles at home never mind two TV's, so playing them was limited to when your dad was at work or a Saturday morning when your parents stayed in bed to have a well-earned lye in. Most of us played out on our BMX bikes, mine was blue with yellow pads and yellow mag wheels! If not on our bikes we would have disappeared into the nearby woods to make dens and campfires, or we would have been cutting wood with our sheath knives and making homemade bow and arrow sets. Nobody gave us a second look, it was normal to see a kid with a knife, no one ever got stabbed, why would they? If you cut yourself or got a splinter you bound it up with whatever you had and walked home so your mum could sort it out or you left it till later if it wasn't that serious. I strolled into the house covered in mud, grass stains and even blood at times after a day out playing, my mum would have rolled her eyes in despair and then stripped me off at the door before sending me off for a bath, my clothes went in the washing machine and were ready for me to get dirty again the next day. As a parent myself now I understand the pressure we are under to keep our kids safe, but I still advocate that a little bit of healthy neglect can really help with a child's development, teach them to build a fire, let them use a saw and teach them to handle a knife safely. Both of my children have shot rifles and have helped me skin animals so they're ready to be cooked, and then they have eaten what we have prepared, Pigeon breast and chips was very popular in my house at one point.

I had always wanted to be a Soldier, so I joined the local Royal Marine Cadets at 13, I was small and thin and looked like a 10 year old. The cadet leaders didn't believe how old I was when I went to join so I had to get proof of my age and embarrassingly my dad had to come down with my birth certificate. At this point my life changed, I had been used to my mum and dad and a few teachers as role models in my life. Well now I had ex Royal Marines with questionable moral compasses and dodgy Navy types with tobacco stained fingers and chests full of WW2 medals. These guys were not our parents and turned a blind eye to our escapades; so swearing, drinking and chasing girls was ok by them, they even took a kick back off some of the stuff we stole. They were the most inappropriate of role models, but they taught us so much.

Telford was a new town and an overspill for the West Midlands, it drew families from other areas of the country too, like us they were in search of a new life and new opportunities. The cadets travelled across the country to go on various camps where we learnt how to be soldiers and sailors, learning skills like camouflage and concealment, how to navigate and how to shoot 7.62mm rifles. I spent weeks away in the long summers on the south coast as boat's crew on a sailing or powerboat course, or would have been found climbing the mountains of Snowdonia whilst learning advanced navigation skills. We had national fieldcraft competitions to test our military skills, we also had sporting events where we swam or played football against cadet units from all over the country. You could have also found us on a drill square in our best 'blues' uniforms, at this regional competition we were judged on our fresh white peaked caps, razor sharp pressed uniforms, polished 'brasses' on our white belts and our shiny 'bulled' boots that looked like mirrors! We were also judged on our ability to do 'foot drill' with and without a rifle, our boots crunched in unison as we marched across the square and our hands were red raw from the impact of slapping them against the rifle as we 'presented arms' for the 100th time that day. This instilled in us standards of discipline, the ability to work as a team and the ability to take orders and execute them with precision! A bi-product of this was a great feeling of pride and confidence in our own abilities as both an individual and as part of a team, these are values that have stayed with me and served me well throughout my whole life.

One of our cadet instructors used to work on the Royal Marines unarmed combat display team during his service, he decided we needed to toughen up and that it was a good idea to put us to work and created his own cadet display team. We were children who were being trained in lethal fighting skills that were meant for use by 'Commando's' to kill an enemy with great efficiency! This punishing regime went on endlessly night after night and even at weekends till our muscles ached and gave up. The display was expertly choreographed with different strangle holds, arm locks and ways to disarm and kill a sentry with a 'Commando Dagger'! The display toured around the country to various British Legion events and county fairs, they happily paid for the privilege of seeing teenagers kick the crap out of each other and attack each other with wooden daggers with great vigour. The instructors used some of the money to get drunk in the bar or the beer tent in between shows, left unsupervised we strutted around the county fair in our sharply pressed uniforms chatting up girls or casing out display tents that we went back to at night to steal from. Our favourite target was the competition tent where keen winemakers and bakers left the homemade wine and cakes, these would have usually been judged by a local dignitary like the mayor or a chinless Member of Parliament after a free lunch, the winner got a rosette and a picture in the local paper. I can only imagine the upset this caused when the competitors returned in the morning and found their prized wine and Victoria sponges gone! We awoke in the morning with empty wine bottles and half eaten cakes in our tents, and as some kind of twisted justice we also had blinding hangovers, which are not much fun at any age, but at 14 years old it's a whole new life experience of pain and nausea! Vows of 'never again' were made but they were short lived goals and we repeated the process for the rest of our lives.

This began a few of us onto a path of crime, we didn't see it as crime though, our childish minds saw it as 'Commando Raids'. We put the same amount of planning and preparation into it as an actual military operation, we wore camouflage gear and use concealment to approach our targets, we posted sentries as lookouts and explored our target looking for something of value to take. My plundering continued even when I was on my own, when I was bored at night you would have found me walking the streets looking for an opportune target like an unlocked car to steal loose change or music cassettes from. When we were at a Military base with cadets we would have searched out a storeroom that was easily accessible to steal kit from for the cadet unit, we never considered this as theft, this was redistribution of resources and 'scavenging' was a military tradition! Being a good scavenger in the British Military, who are often under resourced, has always been a badge of honour and it often served to feed hungry soldiers or give them the equipment they need to live more comfortably; it is only a badge of dishonour if you get caught! Our unit was poor and we didn't have much funding from the Navy, unlike the Army cadets who had no shortage of uniforms, weapons and really good training camps. If we wanted something we had to raise funds or 'redistribute' it from somewhere else! Once whilst visiting another cadet unit our instructors stole a whole sailing boat, trailer included, they just hitched it up to our minibus and we just drove off with it, thus was the example of our leaders and role models!

MINI COMMANDO'S

Our crime wave continued as we travelled the country to attend training weekends, on one such occasion at an Army Field Training Camp some determined and curious cadets came across an insecure storeroom marked as 'visiting unit stores', this was nothing more than an old World War 2 round topped corrugated iron hut, this storeroom belonged to a unit of Territorial Army Reserve Soldiers who were using the same facilities as us at the weekend. The window was insecure and an open invite for a visit from our 'Mini Commandos'. A smaller cadet was soon passed through the window by his mates and once inside he found it to be full of sleeping bags, they were Army issued, the feather lined green roll up ones, a real prize score to a cadet! We only had the cheap camping shop sleeping bags at the unit, so as these would have made our lives in the field more comfortable, they became fair game for redistribution! The cadets formed a chain and passed about 20 sleeping bags out, that was enough for the raiding party to have one each and have a few left over which went back to our stores for other cadets to use. There was an open field nearby and the 'Mini Commando's' had the great idea of making backward footprints in the soft mud, they also discarded a sleeping bag and some other bits along the route too, by doing this they hoped it looked like someone from the nearby town had been in through the insecure boundary and were responsible for the theft. True to form our inappropriate adult instructor took his gift of a nice warm sleeping bag and hid the rest in the mini bus so we could remain undetected. The training event came to an end, and with hope that we could make a clean break we drove towards the exit gates of the camp. An explosion of shouting came from a red faced and very angry looking Colour Sergeant who was gathering his flock of 'weekend warriors' around him, he had noticed the missing sleeping bags and they began to search the camp. The camp was now in 'lockdown' and we were held at the gates in a queue of traffic! The knot in the stomach turned as I considered what would happen if they searched us and found the sleeping bags in our vehicle, what would we say? Our adult would have surely got the most blame and would have been arrested? The 'Mini Commando's' would have to confess and say he knew nothing about it!

   "Right you lot!" Commanded our instructor, **"These are our sleeping bags from our stores, just stick to that story, in fact say nothing and leave it to me",** this was obviously not his first rodeo!

   With bated breath we waited… it felt like an age, the knot in the stomach continued to tighten!

   The footprint scam appeared to have done the job! They had soon found them and the discarded equipment in the field too, the Colour Sergeant put the theft down to civilians from the nearby town. The 'lockdown' was lifted and we drove out of the camp gates, in unison we breathed a sigh of relief that we hadn't been searched, and as was tradition, we lifted the mood and killed time on the journey home by singing rude songs that would have made a sailor blush.

BUSTED!

Eventually as with anything that is fun, it comes to an end,

The 'Wrekin' is an impressive looking hill that erupts out of the Shropshire landscape and can be seen for miles around, it is always the first thing you see as you drive into Telford which sits in its shadow. The Wrekin is a large wooded hill that raises up 407 metres in height, nearly 200 Metres short of being classed as a mountain. The hills steep gradients made it an ideal location for an Iron age fort, with its punishing inclines and dominating views our Iron Age fore fathers would have seen any attackers coming from miles away. On this particular spring day myself and 4 friends decided to climb to the top for no other reason than to be out in the wilds enjoying the company of our mates, we cycled out on our adventure and when we got there we hid our bikes in the woods. Our ascent to the top of our mini mountain on foot began and although we were young and fit the steep gravelly inclines up through 'Hells Gate' and then the more subtle climb through 'Heaven's Gate' wore us out! I could see why our Iron Age fore fathers had chosen this place to fend off attackers. The sweat poured off us and five tired soles took a break at the top by the trig point, we chatted in the sun without a care in the world, we were just enjoying our freedom and pointing out places of interest like where each other lived or where other landmarks were off in the distance. After a well-deserved water break we threw ourselves down the steep back end of the hill, the terrain was unstable, gravelly and root infested underfoot so we used the large trees to break our descent. Once we reached the bottom we walked around the base to the rifle range, it had been there for years, we had even shot there a few times with cadets firing 7.62mm Parker Hale rifles. The range was a well-groomed 1km length of grass with firing points for 12 shooters at every 100 metres, at the top end against the hill was the 'Butts'. This was where the timber and paper targets, usually of a charging soldier, were hoisted up on metal cages by soldiers who were hidden below. They were protected in a bunker type area to protect them from the bullets that 'cracked' as they passed at supersonic speed overhead before crumpling to a halt in the sand embankment beyond. We paused there for a while and dug about in the sand looking for bullet heads to take as souvenirs, the less deformed and battered the better. We found a few and pocketed them, our attention then moved down range and we sauntered down the gravel track that led from the 'Butts' down the treeline. We checked the firing points in case there were some empty bullet cases left behind that the soldiers had failed to see during their clean up, we could have put the bullet heads in them and make a full bullet which was a prized souvenir.

At the end of the track was a single storey white corrugated iron and timber range hut. This was a golden opportunity to nick some military kit to add to our growing collection of stolen booty.

The brass padlocks that held the window shutters closed **'popped'** open as we smashed at them with some bricks that we found nearby on the gravel floor. '**SMASH!**' the window frames followed and shattered into a thousand pieces of white painted timber and plate glass! We climbed in over the broken debris, the inside smelt of stale dust and mouldy paper from the targets that were stored within. We started opening dust covered cabinets and drawers in a frantic search for something of value, we found some old field telephones for use on the range, more targets and a first aid kit, none of these things remotely interested us. I picked up a bunch of keys as I wanted a 'break in bunch', this was a selection of keys that could fit any number of locks to assist in breaking into other places without causing damage, the owner may not even know you had been in their property, perfect for a little thief like me!

"RRRUUUUUUNNNNNN!!!!" Came the shout from outside! We had been rumbled!

I felt my lungs exploding as I hauled myself through the thick spikey hawthorn bushes that lined the ditch I had just vaulted across. The hawthorns dug into my hands and grazed against my legs through my trousers. Hedgerows became boggy fields and my feet became weighed down by thick clay mud that clung to my boots as they sank into the ruts of the field. I saw white police cars patrolling on nearby lanes and I heard van doors crashing shut. Then I heard the deep barking of a large dog, probably a German Shepherd, I knew enough to know the dogs were going to be on our trail in no time! The last thing I wanted was a German Shepherd biting me on my arse and I decided that enough was enough, my mates were covered in mud and looking as sorry for themselves as I felt. It was time to make a move! I struck out from cover onto the main road, it looked deserted at this point and we needed to get to our bikes and make our escape. I was tired, hungry and covered in freezing cold mud, this is usually when people make mistakes, we should have stayed in cover and waited it out. Cops can be lazy and don't want to get dirty, some just want to do the minimum and go home on time, if we were lucky, if we had lazy cops and if we had hidden long enough, we may have got away with it… By going on the road I had made a fatal mistake!

First I heard the acceleration of the engines then the brakes screeching to a halt on the gravel and tarmac surface. We now had two police cars and a police van blocking us from escaping. I think the Police were expecting the IRA or some paramilitary unit as they looked disappointed to see a bunch of 14 year old kids in combat gear. The range was a military location and the IRA had been active in mainland UK at the time, the Police had been told that the suspects were dressed in military clothing and the balloon had gone up! The whole police force had turned out to get some of the action to find out it was 5 kids playing

Soldiers. I was grabbed by a tall police officer who held me roughly by the left arm! I considered making a break for it but he had a vice like grip and his hand dug into my bicep which I thought was going to explode at any minute! He was too strong and before I knew it I was handcuffed! Before we knew what was happening we were secured in the van and the journey to custody had begun. I was crapping myself as my dad was a Policeman and he worked at the station we were heading for at the time. The Custody Sergeant soon clocked the family name and reminded me of the shit I was in… Like I didn't know! What I didn't know at the time was that this was a Burglary, quite a serious offence, I didn't know that! I was just out messing about with my mates, not a real criminal!

My clothing was stripped from me and bagged for evidence, my hair was combed through for glass samples which were collected on a large piece of white paper which was folded up and again sealed in a bag, I was then fingerprinted, photographed and put back into my cell. The room was a standard custody cell with cold whitewashed walls and a black painted concrete floor, there was a fixed bench with a plastic mattress that made you sweat and I stuck to it as I tried in vain to get comfortable, the metal toilet had no seat for comfort and no screen for privacy. The detention staff can check on you through spy holes both in the wall and in the door, which also has a flap for passing food through. It is a de humanising experience but I wasn't scared or emotional, what did upset me was the whispering going on around the custody block between the cops, my dad worked with them and I had become a hot topic of station gossip. This would have embarrassed my dad and I knew it was my mum that was going to pick up the pieces, my dad was going to just close down on me, I'd get a bollocking but beyond that he would have just ignored me, it was his way. He had never been violent to me so I wasn't expecting a beating, maybe I deserved one this time? I didn't know what was going to happen next, I was just knackered so I decided to go to sleep,

I would deal with the fallout when I got home, there was no changing what had happened so why worry about it.

A few hours later I was taken out of the cell and interviewed by two uniformed police officers who looked like they had better things to be doing.

"You do not have to say anything! But it may harm your defence if you do not mention, when questioned something you later rely on in court! Anything you do say may be given in evidence!" the interviewer explained...

'Court' I thought... shit, I'm going to jail! The consequences of what we had done were beginning to dawn on me. I had to try and play this down I thought, just make myself look like a stupid kid, it wasn't hard! The questions began, one of the officers took notes and the other asked the questions,

Q   "Why did you do it?"
A   "Dunno, just messing about"
Q   "What was your intention when you went in the building?"
A   "Just wanted to go in and have a look around"
Q   "Why did you take the keys?"
A   "I just picked them up and shoved them in my pocket when we ran off, I've got no use for them"

I continued with my charade of dopey innocence, I knew what I was doing, I went in there to steal anything of value that I could get my hands on... I was a thief!

They probed my answers and took full advantage of my naivety and lack of legal representation, my mum was my appropriate adult, and her brief was

"Admit what you've done, tell them who you were with and you'll get a 'caution'".

This was an easy way out, a warning that stayed with me until I was 17, all I had to do was admit what I had done and I was going be spared a court appearance and the threat of jail! So under orders I promptly grassed myself and my mates up… it turns out we all got offered the same deal and grassed each other up, we were mates so nobody got any grief for it and we knew there was no honour amongst thieves!

Luckily we weren't kicked out of cadets, as they felt partly responsible I suppose? The adult instructors who had previously turned a blind eye to our escapades wanted to help us, and by kicking us out they would have just abandoned us. We would have been loose on the streets and most definitely have got in a lot more trouble. They taught me an important lesson about looking after your team and not writing people off just because they have made a mistake.

Our scrape with the law came at just the right time, our parents and mentors had been shocked into the reality of what our potential futures looked like if we were not steered back on course. I was given more responsibility and gained rank in the cadets; I made it to the dizzy heights of Corporal, and my parents sent me on every cadet training camp that was out of town in an attempt to keep me occupied in the summer holidays. I wasn't sure if it was a punishment, but we were entered into harder and more strenuous competitions, this included the gruelling and misleadingly named 'Adventure Training' competition on Dartmoor. This was a week of forced marches with heavy rucksacks on; moving from check point to check point across the most inhospitable terrain which was usually reserved for Royal Marine basic training. The only instructors we saw were at the checkpoints and they just gave us our next 8 figure grid reference and sent us off to our next check point, usually up a hill, and in the direction we had just come from. This gruelling event was more akin to SAS selection than any 'Adventure Training' I could imagine… We were being groomed for greater things; out of the 5 of us arrested that day two of them served in the Royal Marines and are now fire fighters, one became an accomplished Chef and I joined the Army and then became a Police Officer. Unfortunately one of our band of desperados fell through the cracks of support and positive role models that the rest of us had in our lives, he continued on a path that led him to jail. I am still in touch with him and you cannot find a nicer guy, his days of being a rogue are over and he is a true gentleman who I am still proud to call a friend. I often wonder what would have become of us if we had been left to hang out on the streets with no positive outlet for our youthful exuberance. This is probably one of those moments those inappropriate role models understood what could become of us, and I thank them for giving us a second chance.

WOOFER!

(A foot soldier of the Worcestershire & Sherwood Foresters Regiment)

'CRACK... RAT, TAT, TAT, TAT', The sound of small arms fire echoed around the streets of Strabane! Nick, the team commander screamed out **"TAKE COVER!!!"** ... As I dived for cover I heard Nick on his radio reporting a calm and controlled **"CONTACT... WAIT OUT!!!"** I made my weapon ready and heard the cocking action of 3 other rifles as we prepared to engage an enemy!

We had been on night patrols in the border town of Strabane, and we had been making our way back to our patrol base at the 'Hump' vehicle check point where our beds were waiting for us. It had been a long cold night and we were done in! The Provisional Irish Republican Army (PIRA) knew this too, they had probably had 'dickers' out all night watching us and knew that we were near to hand over time, so a perfect time to unleash their attack on the nearby Police Station.

I had only just joined the Battalion after basic training and because I was only 17, I had to be kept in camp until my 18th Birthday! We were in Northern Ireland as part of Op Banner which was the name of the military operation to support the civilian authorities in Northern Ireland, this was a Police led campaign and due to this any soldier on the streets had to be over the age of 18. On my birthday I was assigned to 6 Platoon in B Company where I was introduced to my team or 'brick' as it was known. The Commander was Nick, a Corporal who was a no-nonsense kind of leader, his pale skin and thinning red hair mixed with a short temper made him someone I was fearful of. I had nothing to fear from him though, he had found out that one of the senior guys in the platoon had been physically abusing me, so with his special kind of tact and diplomacy he made sure that there was no repeat of it, I knew this was someone who would look after me! Baldrick was the senior soldier, a tall lad from up Sheffield way, he had a friendly way about him and was like a big brother. Then we had George! George was now senior to me in the 'brick' as I took his place as the 'sprog', but this was as far as it went, George was a lovely guy but was as soft as a puppy and daft as a brush.

There are 3 'bricks' to a 'multiple', this allowed us to patrol an area with great flexibility, one 'brick' that gave overwatch and cover whilst the others did vehicle check points or carried out a search of an area. It also allowed cut off teams to use alley ways and side roads to intercept snipers if the other bricks came under attack.

I was the new guy, the 'sprog' so I had the heavier LSW (Light Support Weapon) it was the job of the 'sprog' to have this weapon, and George, the previous owner handed it over with a big grin on his face, he was no longer the 'Sprog', he had now been promoted by virtue of seniority. I didn't mind though, it had a longer and tougher barrel that gave accurate and higher rates of fire and it had bipod legs to give it more stability, to me it felt like the superior of the two SA80 rifle variants! I also had the pleasure of carrying the team 'Baton Gun', a basic tube of metal with a trigger mechanism and a metal rifle butt, this was used to fire the 37mm rubber bullets that were used to disperse rioters. We were also issued Improved Northern Ireland Body Armor (INIBA) with extra tough plates front and rear that covered your heart to protect against a sniper shot, the body armor had a distinct fusty smell, a mix of sweat and Kevlar that every infantryman knows. I had packed enough kit for 4 weeks of operations in my rucksack. Or 'Bergan' as it is known and had six 30 round magazines of 5.56mm ammunition in my ammo pouches as well as the ammunition for the baton gun.

The multiple loaded onto a PUMA helicopter and flew out from the Battalion HQ in Omagh! We cut low across the countryside, or 'cuds' as the old sweats called it, 'hedgehopping' low only popping up briefly to avoid power cables, and then back to the deck into a contour hugging flight. This was necessary to avoid any fire from some of the Anti-Aircraft weaponry that PIRA had recently used against our helicopters. After 30minutes of a stomach-churning flight we landed in a dust bowl on the edge of Strabane, the helicopters kept their engines running and rotors turning as we unloaded our kit, once empty the helicopters lifted leaving us hugging the ground in a dust storm as they clattered away. I saw a short distance away a concrete and corrugated iron fortress on the border, this was to be my home for the next 4 weeks.

Strabane is a Border Town in West Tyrone which sat on the junction of three rivers, The Mourne river in the North of Ireland which dissected the town of Strabane in two and the rivers Finn and Foyle which acted as the border into the republic of Ireland. A long road bridge led from the 'Hump' into the Irish town of Lifford, the customs check point was called the 'Hump' for no other reason than it was built on a hump in the road… Irish logic I suppose? The town was split into three main areas; Strabane Town Centre, which wasn't massive, it had rows of terrace streets and a shopping area which was busy in the day with banks a supermarket and a few clothes shops. On the weekends the night life was quite eventful and the town came to life, with the boys all boozed up and the girls dressed to impress. whilst on patrol we often passed through the town, you could smell the cigarette smoke and beer from the bars and every so often you got a whiff of perfume from a passing girl, it made us long to be home and out on the town ourselves. Inevitably some drunk lads saw us, usually on the main street square where the local lads got drunk on cheap booze before going into the pub. The mood rapidly changed, bottles were thrown, and someone always came out raging at us and wanting to fight a Brit Soldier, we always obliged. This was a tipping point and crowds of angry and drunk Republican supporters came out of the bars to join the ruckus, inevitably more bottles and bricks were thrown. Eventually we had to either withdraw or Baton Rounds (rubber bullets) were fired to disperse the crowd!

Further out of town you had a small estate known as the Head of Town, it was a rundown council estate of no more than 5 streets nestled in a valley. This place was dangerous to us, it was a stronghold of anti-British sentiment in the town, they flew Irish Republican flags from the lampposts and painted the kerb stones on the road edges the green, white and orange of the Irish flag. Known 'Terrorists' lived here, and they had the power of life and death over every person on that estate, every house was a safe house for them. There were Murals on the gable ends of houses and on large walls all celebrating the fight against the Brits. The nearby cemetery was used to lay to rest IRA volunteers who died for the cause. Even the children hated us, and kids of all ages came out when we were on the streets to throw insults at us and lob a few bricks from the derelict houses.

Across the bridge you had the 'Ballycolman' estate, this was a large estate and also a hot bed of Republican activity. It too had the large mural paintings on the walls and a general distain for Brit soldiers. But on this estate people kept themselves to themselves and rarely came out for trouble. I recall being crouched in cover by a garden gate one day on Bridge Street, when an old lady surreptitiously walked over to me, she looked down at me and I looked up to meet her gaze from under my helmet, she had a kind face and was no threat.

"AH you remind me of my grandson, god bless ya" she purred out in a soft Irish accent,

she then discreetly palmed me a couple of wrapped humbug sweets, like your nan does when she slips you a £10 note when you're broke, this was an act of humanity I will never forget! However, I couldn't take the risk of eating them and potentially being poisoned, so when she had gone I discreetly discarded them down a storm drain.

***

Strabane Police Station was the hub of the local Royal Ulster Constabulary (RUC), it was a large building on the area known as the 'bowling green'. The station was also a fortress of concrete blocks and corrugated iron, there were watch towers and rocket nets designed to catch the blast of any rocket propelled grenades before they were able to harm anyone.

At the time we had heard the shots ringing out an RUC vehicle patrol had been checking out Church View, a road situated on high ground behind the station and therefore a potential threat area where an attack was likely to be mounted from. These patrols were called Mortar Baseplate Patrols and were designed to deter attacks!

The plain blue armored Ford Sierra Police car drove onto church view, it was a single-track road with alleys leading off to the rear of the houses on the left, to the right was a clear view down to the RUC station. Ahead the two officers saw a dirty silver Toyota Hiace van, it was doing what appeared to be a three-point turn in the road between a gap in the houses. The driver of the van had his face covered and when he saw the RUC approach he froze in his seat, only turning his head to talk into the rear of the van! The back doors of the van opened, and a second man emerged, this one was wearing a combat jacket and a black balaclava covering his face and head, he walked backwards with his arms tight into his body towards the approaching Police car. After 3 paces he turned and dropped to one knee, as he did this, he bought up into a firing position an AK47 rifle which he levelled into an aim at the approaching Police Officers. Without pause or warning he fired the rifle… **'CRACK'**, that was the first shot we had heard! The 7.62mm round he had fired at the Police Officers had found its target as the drivers wing mirror shattered into pieces, the Terrorists second shot never came! The rifle had jammed, and he began to cock the handle back and fumble with the magazine release catch to clear the weapon. This gave the Police Officers an opportunity! The driver, not knowing what they were facing put the vehicle in reverse to escape, the passenger opened his door and pointed his 9mm Sub Machine Gun out and sprayed rounds in the direction of the Terrorists!… **'Rat, tat, tat, tat'** that was the second burst of shots we had heard! This return fire from the Police Officer was enough to deter the Terrorists who fled into the alley ways that led to the 'Head of Town' estate, they were there to fire a mortar, not engage in a firefight, their mission was complete.

The improvised mortar they left behind was intended for the Police Station at handover time! It would have been a significant victory for the IRA cause if it had been successfully fired into a busy Police Station, thankfully the 'mortar' landed within the compound but failed to explode! These were homemade devices that were fabricated from large gas bottles and they were very unreliable, often failing to explode. They were however an important part of the IRA's arsenal and if deployed correctly, it would have caused many deaths and injuries!

The **'CONTACT'** from the Police Officers had made its way across the radio waves and we were sent into the 'Head of Town' to capture or kill the fleeing Terrorists! Nick gathered us all up off the sodden wet floor where we had been awaiting orders and gave us a quick brief on what we were to do! **"Transports down on the road and we are going to the head of town! We are to clear the** area between the RUC Station and out the edge of town, they are armed so be careful and don't take any chances."

When I say 'Transport' I meant a knackered old white escort van we had in the compound. Daz from the intelligence unit had it for mooching about in so he was able to move from base to base covertly. Daz screeched out of the gates of the 'Hump' like something out of a 70's Police car chase and loaded 12 hairy arsed soldiers fully kitted and fully armed into the back of the van! As you can imagine the van struggled to get up any great speed, but it still lurched from side to side as we made progress through the town. This and the musty smell of 12 damp soldiers in the back of the van did nothing to alleviate the feelings of nausea.

Our search began as we worked our way up hill through the Convent school grounds to the rear of Church View. The adrenaline was up and the weight of my kit became insignificant, we moved forward in pairs to cover each other, the morning air was cold and burnt in my throat and chest leaving a metallic blood taste!

"Move!" George and I moved to cover,

"Move!" Nick and Baldrick moved… "Move…Move… Move."

It continued as we bounced forward in pairs, it was hard work and whilst static we scanned ahead for threats, if we were fired on the whole team wouldn't be exposed and we could return accurate and suppressing fire. As we reached the tree line at the top of the hill I realized how tired I was now feeling! I had just completed a 10-hour night patrol and was long overdue food and sleep. My arms and body ached as I was still getting used to carrying a rifle, body armor and all the extra heavy bits of kit we were issued with. As the 'sprog' I had to carry anything that nobody else wanted to carry, and Nick had spent the last week growling at me for not carrying my rifle high enough in a correct patrol manner with the rifle butt in my shoulder. This 'Alert' position is used so that the weapon can be bought up into the aim and fired instantly, however my weak arms often let it drop to my hips when no one was watching. I was definitely in the 'Alert' position now!

We patrolled along the high ground on the outskirts of the 'Head of Town', Sweat ran down my face and stung my eyes, the leather pad inside my helmet was soaked and the straps dug into my chin. The cool wind on this high ground was a welcome relief as it cooled the sweat on my body, we remained in the cool wind on the high ground and observed the streets below, we had no intention of going down there, there may be booby traps on the alleys or a sniper lying in wait! If the Terrorists had gone to ground, they were for sure having a cup of tea and a few biscuits in one of the many safehouses that lay beneath us… They were gone, they were like Wolves that had disappeared into the safety of their lair!

We moved back from the high ground to reorganize in the grounds of the Convent, Baldrick who was ever the optimist knocked on the large wooden doors and was greeted by a Nun.

"Hello me duck, any chance of a cuppa???" he asked in his cheekiest northern accent,

"NO" came a sharp reply as the large wooden door was slammed shut in his face! you can't beat a bit of Christian kindness, can you!

The weeks continued and I began to get used to the hours of pounding the street. My feet were no longer sore, and my arms and shoulders had become used to the heavy rifle and kit that I was carrying. I learnt the town layout, where were the most dangerous areas and where previous attacks had taken place. The faces of the local IRA and INLA terrorists or 'players' also became familiar as we conducted our frequent 'stop searches' on them. They too got to know us and one remarked on how young I looked,

"**Ah it's such a shame that a wee child like you is to be sent here to be killed!**" he said sarcastically as I searched him.

As I recall, I told him to **"GO FUCK YOURSELF PADDY"** then tapped my rifle and gave him a cheeky wink, showing I was happy for them to try!

We left Strabane as we had arrived, on a stomach-churning cross-country helicopter ride. I believe our replacements were greeted by another IRA Mortar attack, but this time it was at the 'Hump', luckily, it again failed to detonate and landed next to my old friend John Connaughton who was sheltering under a table!

PROXY BOMB

We returned to Omagh to continue our cycle of duties, we were now moving into 'Guards and Parties' which was when we lived in the main camp and did guard duty or got drunk in the NAAFI. Lisanelly Barracks was a large camp that sprawled out on the edge of Omagh City and was flanked by the River Strule. It had numerous barrack blocks or company lines as they were known, enough to house a whole battalion. There was a cookhouse to feed us and a couple bars dotted about to keep us lubricated, and we also had a large gymnasium and PT staff to make sure we didn't get too fat and lazy. Guard duty consisted of manning the various look outposts known as 'Sangers' or guarding the front gate to control access to the camp. We also carried out perimeter patrols to prevent security breaches through the fence. If you weren't on guard You were pretty much free to do what you wanted and that mostly involved getting drunk. In the evening the NAAFI bar began to fill up, and a hardcore of drinkers went to a bar called the 'plastic pig', which was known for late night lock ins. This was a black and white prefabricated bungalow sized building with mock Tudor beams on the outside. On the inside it had the feel of a real English pub, with more mock beams and horse brasses attached for that old look, it also had a pool table in the centre that was always in use. There was also a family's bar in the married quarters called the White Hart, but this was usually out of bounds to single soldiers to prevent us from having affairs with married women whilst their husbands were deployed on operations. The drinking was continuous, heavy and destructive, it was quite normal for fights to break out or to see soldiers vomiting in the toilets or outside on the road. As the bars shut we bought a takeaway crate of beer each and continue drinking in the accommodation block, Holsten Pilsner was my tipple of choice. Block parties consisted of taking over one of the larger accommodation rooms where we played loud music, drank crates of beer and watched pornographic videos on loop as background entertainment. Games like 'Dambusters' were played, this involved player stripping naked and placing a 2 pence coin between their butt cheeks, they then negotiated various obstacles placed in their way along the corridor, water was thrown on them too just to disrupt their flight and make them drop the coin. If they made it to the end they had to drop the coin into a pint glass that was sat waiting. It was great fun, but they were also times of danger and people got hurt!

Military accommodation in the late 80's and early 90's, especially in the Infantry, was one of the most dangerous places to live that I know of, it is a place where you can either sink or swim! You have a concentration of young fit men who are trained to kill, and have just returned from stressful operations, they are heavy drinkers and want to party hard and release their aggression. There are initiations for new members of the Platoon that can involve humiliation, assault and dangerous activities like throwing people down stairs in wooden lockers. If it was your turn you just took it on the chin in the knowledge that everyone else in the room had been through the same ordeal! In my experience if things began to get out of hand or if people went too far someone always stepped in, contrary to popular belief malicious bullying was rare! However, if someone had a grudge, and a fight broke out it could have easily ended in a serious assault with the loser ending up in the medical centre with GBH injuries. If you don't have your own private room there is no escape or door to close to lock the animals out! And if the senior guys choose your large shared room for the party then that's what is going to happen! Officers and senior ranks live away from the 'block' and didn't really know about what went on, to them it was just 'Block Life', they had lived through it and they saw it as normal, if you reported things to them you were a 'Grass' and became very unpopular. Like I said you either sink or swim, it was a life we chose! Some of the lads left as they didn't like it, they couldn't stand 'Block Life', as for the rest of us, we got our arm bands on and learnt to swim with the sharks… never fall asleep at a block party is my best advice to the uninitiated, you may be missing eyebrows when you wake up!

***

This respite from operations was not without risk! In the early 90's the IRA carried out attacks on Military and RUC bases using a number of methods; The Sniper, The Mortar and most concerning of all was the 'Proxy Bomb!'.

The Proxy Bomb, or Human Bomb was a savage tactic where civilians and off duty Security Forces staff were forced to drive car bombs into military bases. Their homes were taken over by the IRA and their families were held hostage, the driver was told if he didn't do as he was told their families were to be killed. The driver was strapped into a vehicle full of explosives and told to drive to a military base where the bomb was remotely detonated by the terrorists who were following behind.

24 OCTOBER 1990

On this day 3 synchronised attacks took place at Coshquin (near Derry), Cloghoge (near Newry) and at our camp, Lisanelly Barracks in Omagh! The drivers of the vehicles were deemed to be collaborators with the security services and had had their family's taken hostage. If they failed to deliver the bombs to the targets their families were to be murdered!

I was dressed in my running gear and preparing to walk down to the Gym. I had that uneasy nervous feeling that I always got just before doing a BFT (Battle Fitness Test), it was an irrational nervousness as it was only a mile and a half best effort run in trainers, shorts and T-Shirt. However you were expected to do it in under 10 minutes, if you failed then you got remedial PT!!! Nobody wanted that!!!

All of a sudden I heard panicked shouts out in the stairwell of the accommodation. It was the 'guard' they were evacuating the building,

"Quick, get out and down to the Gym, there's a bomb at the front gate".

The gate was only a couple hundred metres away so I grabbed a warm top and joined the trail of evacuees leaving the accommodation. We were billeted in the Gymnasium building and soon after a stream of soldiers and staff from other parts of the camp joined us.

We hadn't been there too long when we heard the distant **'wuump'** of a bomb detonation!

I feel it is important to give a good account of what happened that day as my involvement was that of an evacuee, and there is very little detail of what actually happened on available research tools. To do this I have contacted some of the soldiers who were there to piece together what happened and I have added some personal accounts below too,

Lance Corporal Mike SMITH had been on duty in a 'Sanger' next to the large black metal gates at the front of the camp. The front gate area was a wide road flanked by blast walls either side of the road. The road itself that led through this area had large concrete blocks strategically placed into a chicane or zig zag to slow down any cars that might try to make a dash into the camp. He was soon to be joined by Private Richardson who was walking across the road to the 'sanger' to complete a handover. A vehicle pulled up to the gate and the heavy metal gate opened, allowing a camper van into the search area to check the driver's identity. The driver was a familiar face, it was 'Shaun', a civilian mechanic who worked in the camp. Shaun's window was partially down and he began shouting,

"THERES A BOMB IN THE BACK GET AWAY".

Richardson didn't need telling twice and retreated at speed to the guardroom to raise the alarm, Mike was now left with a decision to make,

> At around 1am that morning Shaun's home had been invaded and his family taken hostage by IRA terrorists, the family were tied to chairs and held at gun point. Shaun, a catholic man, had the charges read out to him and informed that he was a **'collaborator'** to the Crown Forces. He was informed that the IRA had found him guilty of this charge and had sentenced him to summary execution! This wouldn't be a simple death though; his family camper van was taken away and returned a few hours later with it full of explosives. Such was the hatred and malice of his captors that they used this waiting time to savagely beat him and make threats of harm to his family. They didn't beat him too much though, they needed him to be able to drive. Shaun was tied into the vehicle and told that his family was going to die if he didn't drive the bomb into the Lisanelly Barracks where he worked. He was also told that the van was rigged to blow up if he tried to escape, and they were going to be following him with a remote-controlled detonator. Shaun's death sentence was to become a human bomb!

1500 lbs of Home-Made Explosive known as ANFO had now been driven in through the front gate in Shaun's camper van. ANFO is a mix of ammonium nitrate and fuel oil, and as with all homemade explosives it is temperamental. But if mixed and deployed correctly its effects are devastating, this was shown in the mainland Bombing campaign that devastated the London Stock exchange on the 20th July 1990 and later at the Manchester shopping centre on the 15th June 1996.

Mike SMITH was now faced with the decision to run and leave Shaun or stay and help. Mike really had no choice, time was ticking, he had to do something! With no regard for his own life he opened the driver's door, he saw that Shaun was tied to the seat and began to untie the ropes that held Shaun in place. The ropes became loose and Shaun was set free! Mike pulled him out of the vehicle and across the road to the protection of the blast walls whilst shouting,

"BOMB FRONT GATE, BOMB FRONT GATE".

The area of the bomb was cleared and anyone in offices or accommodation nearby was evacuated away from the area. The QRF or quick reaction force, which at that time was the Machine Gun Platoon from D Company, deployed to the nearby streets to search for possible terrorist suspects and other devices. A cordon was put in place on the main Gortin Road which ran past the front of the camp, these locations were always checked for secondary devices! The IRA were known to stage an attack and then plant a second device at locations where the security forces were likely to set up cordons, the device was then detonated with the intention of killing unsuspecting first responders, or if they were lucky the prize of a bomb disposal officer.

The camper van remained sat there, no explosion… was this a hoax bomb? Was it a faulty device?, had the large metal gates blocked the radio-controlled signal that was meant to detonate the bomb?

Now that cordons had been put in place the bomb disposal teams began to examine the device using the tracked bomb disposal robot, which was fitted with a camera and other sensors to check for booby traps. The ATO (Ammunition technical officer) then went forward in his blast proof suit to confirm it was safe and placed a controlled charge on the bomb so he could detonate it from distance. This was a simple 'pull' device that he would have kept control of until it was safe for him to 'pull' and set off the detonator. As the ATO began to walk the long walk back to safety there was an earth-shaking eruption behind him, he was heard to say, **"Who pulled that?"**. In fact nobody had, there had been a timer hidden in the device! This had only set off a booster pack though, and the bomb had not detonated fully. The blast had sent the ANFO contained in the bomb in all directions littering the road and guardroom roof with debris. Was this the plan all along, to lure the bomb disposal officer in to start diffusing the bomb and then blow them up?

A further 'cook off' period was given to allow for any other timers and then the ATO forensically began to take the device apart. Bomb makers are like Tradesmen or Artists, and they use signature work that can be attributed back to a particular bomb maker. Or they may have been sloppy and left forensics like fingerprints, DNA or other identifiable items that would have led investigators back to a suspect. If the explosives were 'exotic' or commercially made like SEMTEX, it can be tracked back to its source and help to identify countries that were supplying arms to the IRA.

Here is the account of Lt Colonel Mike SMITH who was at the time a young Lance Corporal in the regimental band and on guard duty at the front gate that day,

> *My recollections of the Incident on Oct 24, 1990 – Proxy Bomb, Lisanelly Bks, Omagh.*
>
> *I was on camp guard duty at the front gate vehicle search sanger in Lisanelly Bks, Omagh at the time of the incident. Lee Stokes was in the sangar with me, he was gate man.*
>
> *Prior to going out on stag we were informed there had been two incidents that morning: Coshquin vehicle check point near Londonderry and Cloghoge VCP near Newry. We did not know*

at that point what had happened at those locations, just to be extra vigilant.

It's probably a good thing we didn't know what had happened at both of those incidents.

At around 0630 a red Camper Van drove up to the main gate, as with normal procedure the gate man let the vehicle in through the gates to park between the blast walls. As the driver drove past me he said something in a strong Northern Irish accent which I didn't catch. As I walked up from the rear of the vehicle to the driver's door I noticed there was a lot of straw in the back of the vehicle. He had lowered the window down and I noticed he had been badly beaten, blood coming out of wounds on his face. He then said, *'There's a bomb in the back'*. Given the frequency of guard duties carried out by the band during this time the knowledge of immediate drills was well known by all band members, I opened the vehicle door (not knowing that other vehicles that day had been booby trapped) and on opening the door I noticed he had been tied in with rope to the seat and driving wheel. I untied him (quickly), grabbed him, dragged him out and made my way to the guardroom, shouting **"Bomb Main Gate"**.

The Guardroom cleared very quickly. I hauled the victim to the Ops Room, where I recall the alarm not working even with WOII Burry's best efforts of hitting it really hard.

ATO were called and got to the main gate relatively quickly. They reported after the event that a combination of that gate being closed behind the vehicle and a faulty detonator resulted in the 1500lbs bomb not going off.

Bomb disposal carried out a controlled explosion of the detonator which resulted in the van roof being blown half a mile down the road.

Following the controlled explosion I was interviewed by the military police in a car outside the HQ. Whilst this was happening the Barrack fire alarm went off as one of the accommodation blocks was on fire. One of the soldiers had wet his bed and was attempting to dry his mattress with an electric heater. When they were called out to the muster point it was confirmed that he had left the heater on and the fire had started.

I recall seeing Bandsman Stokes dragging the fire trolley on his own towards the accommodation to try and put the fire out.

I was awarded a Mention in Dispatches, and attended the awards ceremony at Air House, Episkopi the following summer. Since WW2 there has only been one other Musician to have been mentioned in dispatches, Sgt George Mair of the Light Infantry Band for actions during the Gulf War.

I have been informed that there have been reports that the NAAFI manageress was the hero of the day. I can assure all that neither Lee Stokes or myself worked for the NAAFI and that no-one from the NAAFI had anything to do with this incident.

Reading about the other incidents that happened that morning it is a miracle we got away unscathed, things could have been so different.

Here is the account of WOII Chris Burry, watch keeper on duty at the time of the attack,

I paraded for duty at 06:00hrs that morning to relieve WOII "Jock" Gillies who had been on duty overnight. Upon arrival in the Op's room Jock informed me that there had been two attacks on security bases, in Newry and in Londonderry. He informed me that the IRA had used proxy bombs and there had been reports of follow up gun fire. He then said **"we are next"** I made a comment in reply to imply he was joking. Having taken over my duties I asked the signaller to get the kettle on and settled down for my day's work.

It couldn't have been more than 15 minutes later when L/Cpl Michael Smith came into the Op's Room escorting a civilian. He immediately informed me that there was a bomb at the front gate and he, pointing at the civilian, drove it. I responded by saying **"you are fucking joking!"**.

Cpl Smith then went on to explain that the guy had been tied in the van and that he had to cut him free to get him out. The penny soon dropped that this was no joke and I then noticed that the civilian was showing signs of distress and I also saw marks on the guy's wrists where some sort of restraint had been used on him. So I then shouted to the signaller to activate the mortar alarm, he had to climb onto the desk to get to the button which was located high up on the wall. I should say now that this alarm was tested on a weekly basis and it chose that day not to work! I shouted, **"hit the fucking thing"** and jumped up to try to do it myself without success. We now had a situation where we had an attack in progress and no way of alerting the camp. Things got a bit blurred after this but eventually I remember ATO coming into the Op's room where he took a small cigar out of his pocket, broke it in half and lit up. He then commenced interviewing the civilian. I remember him asking what had happened and the guy explaining that the IRA had come to his house after midnight and kept his family hostage whilst they took his camper van away. ATO asked how long they had taken to load the device and he had replied about half an hour. ATO then asked him if the van felt heavy to drive and he replied **"yes"**. It was then that ATO made the follow statement: **"Gentlemen we are just about to get fragged"**. It was not long after this that ATO advised that the Op's room was too close to the front gate and that it was prudent to evacuate to a safer distance from the device. I remember exiting the building from the rear door carrying half a dozen rifles, I think they were the COP platoon weapons that were stored in the op's room. I'm not sure exactly how long after we evacuated the op's room before the device partially functioned.

I have seen posts on Facebook that suggest that the NAFFI manager got the guy out of the van because the band had been on guard and they ran away. I hope this account clarifies what *actually happened. L/Cpl Smith was mentioned in despatches for his actions that day, he is now a Lieutenant Colonel, the director of music for the Grenadier Guards.*

WOII Chris Burry went on to complete 20 years' service with the RUC GC after leaving the Worcestershire and Sherwood foresters.

Another incident that morning, as mentioned by Mike Smith, was a fire in the Headquarters accommodation block! A soldier who will remain known as 'Albert' had had a heavy night of drinking in the bar the night before the attack. In his drunken state he had pissed the bed! Usually you would have to swap your mattress for a new one and would have to pay a bill for it. Now Albert didn't have any money as he had spent it all on beer! So he thought it a good idea to put the sodden mattress over an electric heater in his room to dry out! When the alarm sounded and everyone fled for safety he left the mattress unattended on the heater. The mattress began to smoulder and begun to fill the room with thick black poisonous smoke. The smoke billowed out of the window that had been left open to allow the smell of Alberts drying piss to escape. B Company looked up from the gym bemused at the smoke and we thought that maybe this was bomb damage… it turned out to be an own goal by a bed wetter called 'Albert'!

Also two of the Battalions motorised transport platoon, both characters who liked a drink, where conspicuous in their absence during this incident. It appears Frank Cain and Gary Baker had been on an all-night drinking session in the 'plastic pig' and were trapped in the pub throughout the whole incident… some people get all the luck!

B Company were quite happy at the time that they had missed their fitness test. However it was rescheduled for later that afternoon, there was no escaping that! I made it in under 10 minutes too thus avoiding remedial PT!!!

On a serious note, of the 3 proxy bombs deployed by the IRA that day,

The first at Coshquin (near Derry) a 42 year old catholic man by the name of Patrick Gillespie was chained into a van and drove a 1000 lb bomb into the permanent border checkpoint on Buncrana Road. Gillespie and five soldiers were killed, including Kingsman Stephen Beacham, Vincent Scott, David Sweeney, Paul Worrall and Lance Corporal Stephen Burrows, from D (Support) Company of the 1st Battalion the King's Regiment.

the second at Cloghoge (near Newry) a 65 year old Catholic Man by the name of James McAvoy was forced to drive a van into a permanent vehicle check point at Cloghoge. One of the terrorists must have felt some guilt and he was warned not to open the doors as they were booby trapped and to escape out of the window. Just short of his target McAvoy stopped the van and escaped through his window. This alerted a soldier who shouted at him to move the van, the van exploded killing Ranger Cyril J. Smith, from B Company, 2nd Battalion the Royal Irish Rangers! The explosion also injured 13 other soldiers and McAvoy suffered a broken leg. Ranger SMITH was posthumously awarded the Queens Gallantry Medal for raising the alarm rather than running for cover.

The name of the driver at the third Proxy bomb in Omagh is not easily found through reasonable research, potentially due to fear for his safety, I have used a pseudonym for ease of reading and to respect his privacy if that is what he wishes. To my knowledge there were no serious injuries due to the only partial detonation of the device. Lance Corporal SMITH was awarded a Mention in Dispatches for his bravery.

After the atrocities of the 24th October 1990 there was uproar and indignation from within the catholic community and the use of 'Human Bombs' was abandoned by the IRA!

***

I look back and at 18 years old I would have loved to of been the heroic soldier who came under fire and bravely killed a terrorist, Maybe even got a medal for it! But now I'm glad that never happened. In recent years veterans of the 'troubles' have been investigated by the Historical Enquiries Team (HET), which was commissioned by the Police Service of Northern Ireland (PSNI). The role of the HET was to examine all deaths attributable to the security situation that occurred in Northern Ireland between 1968 when the Army was first deployed to assist in the escalating violence, and the Belfast Agreement, also known as the Good Friday Agreement in 1998. Old soldiers, many of whom were in poor health have faced prosecution for incidents that had happened over 40 years ago. On the flip side there had been early releases from jail and letters telling terrorist suspects that we had no interest in detaining them or prosecuting them for their offences in the interests of peace.

The IRA was also riddled with informants! They were handled by MI5 and Special Branch but to maintain their cover they still took an active part in IRA activity. By adopting this tactic many Soldiers lives were saved by 'faulty' devices or countermeasures like overt patrols or ambushes to frustrate IRA activity. One such individual was reported in the media as Declan 'Beano' Casey from Strabane! CASEY was a self-confessed IRA member and had been outed as an Informant or 'Supergrass' for the security services in Northern Ireland in the late 80's and early 90's. Without a doubt he is the type of individual I will have stop searched on a frequent basis and have done nothing more than reinforced his cover story as a man of the IRA. If I had come up against him during a terrorist attack I would have treated him like my enemy and would have shown him no mercy. But due to the information he supplied many lives were saved, had this individual been killed by soldiers responding to an attack it could have caused unknown damage to the intelligence picture we had of the IRA. He was our informant and the information he supplied was worth more than a moment of glory for a young soldier. He was playing big boy's games in a dirty war where both sides did things of questionable morality and a source like this was expendable if the bigger picture dictated it. And as we know when you play big boy's games you have to play by big boy's rules, he knew the risks and I wonder what his motivations were?

But what is for sure is that the British Secret Service's had infiltrated the IRA right up to the highest of their leadership. They knew that the only way forward was by peaceful political means, so they played both sides of the fence in a hope to secure a deal.

I look back and reflect on my time in Northern Ireland where I served 3 tours of duty in all, I conclude that had I grown up in a town like Strabane as a young Catholic man, I too would have been an IRA volunteer! I cannot imagine my children growing up in a world where armed soldiers roamed the streets stopping and searching who they wanted with no real grounds. Or soldiers stopping your car on a family day out, detaining you and your family on the side of the road where you were held at gun point whilst your car was searched!

I am and always will firm believer that only fools do not respect an enemy like the IRA, and that we should remember that,

'One man's terrorist is another man's freedom fighter!'

JAIL BIRD

I winced with nauseous pain as the sunlight beamed through the iron bars that caged me into a small prison cell, I blinked my eyes open and felt the hard dusty floor beneath me, I paused and considered to myself **"Where the fuck am I?"**

The hard floor was no worse than the countless floors I had slept on as a soldier but this one came with a bite, literally! I had ant bites all up the right side of my body which had been left exposed for the ants to nip at throughout last night. I stood up and stretched out my arms, I then dipped my body either side to stretch out my side muscles, this loosened my back and legs which had cramped after a night on a concrete mattress. I had a stinking hangover, a dry mouth and the smell of alcohol on my breath was only overpowered by the smell coming from the jail that I awoke to find myself in. I stood at the bars looking out onto what I can only describe as a scene from a 'Spaghetti Western' Movie; I was in one of about 8 cells that looked out onto a small tennis court sized exercise yard, the jail was made of stone and plaster which was probably whitewashed at some point, but now it was baked yellow in the Mediterranean sun and was now worn out and crumbling. The exercise yard was enclosed by a 12ft stone wall with an entry point to the yard from a sentry post to my left, the Police Officer at the entry gate was wearing a light blue uniform and was armed with a holstered pistol on his right hip, he also had a long baton hanging from his utility belt on his left side, he was obviously right handed and ready for a cross draw with his baton if he needed it. He was too far behind the gate for anyone to make a grab for the weapons, but I made a mental note of their whereabouts anyway, if we were going to take a beating I was going to go down fighting. Looking up I saw the clear blue sky above but the open top of the exercise yard was crisscrossed with barbed wire to prevent an escape, I took note of that too in case they wanted to keep us here for longer than we wanted to stay... Welcome to the prisoner holding center of Larnaca Police Station!

Larnaca is Cyprus's second largest city after Nicosia, it therefore had a larger prisoner holding area than most of the surrounding towns like Ayia Napa, where Myself, Leggy, Mad Willy and Wiggy had been out the night before partaking in our usual antics of drinking, dancing and trying to find Scandinavian women who were looking for fun. Cyprus was a popular tourist spot in the early 90's for Scandinavian women who wanted sun, sand and sex, they left their boring men at home and chose the company of the 'Crazy British Soldiers' who always had the appetite for fun. Apparently Scandinavian men are quite boring, they have a reserved character that doesn't fit in well in nightclubs, whereas the British Soldiers were always up for a laugh and willing to do crazy things like skinny dipping at 3am after a night on the dance floor, that's what they told us anyway!

The gate to my cell wasn't locked and I saw that there were a few people milling around the yard, most were scruffy Mediterranean men who looked skinny and unwashed, maybe drug addicts or sneak in thieves who targeted holiday makers, or both, I didn't really care. They looked sheepish and avoided any eye contact as I looked around to see who my potential threats might be. I had remembered being bought in the night before and being placed into the cell on my own and hearing someone from the darkness calling out,

JAIL BIRD

"Hello English boys, we will fuck you English boys!"

Obviously full of drink and aggression myself and the lads had given back some typically English replies,

"FUCK YOU, YOU FUCKING CUNTS, WERE THE BRITISH ARMY, COME NEAR US AND YOU'RE FUCKING DEAD!"

I was kind of regretting this show of bravado now that the mix of 'brandy sour' cocktails and 'Keo' beer had worn off a bit. However, this was now a potentially dangerous situation and not the time to go around each cell to apologise for my terrible manners and inexcusable use of foul language, I was a very fresh faced 19 year old and I didn't fancy being someone's Jail bride for the duration of my stay. I was still wearing my suede desert boots, cargo shorts and baggy T-shirt, this was like an off duty uniform for most soldiers stationed in Cyprus, in the UK the only difference would have been jeans rather than the shorts. We had our belts and laces still and the only things that had been taken off us at the charge desk the night before was our wallets. We had been purposefully difficult there too, we had all refused to sign documents that were not printed in English, why would've we signed a document that was written in Greek? It might have been an admission of guilt or an agreement to pay some money. We had all received some training in what to do when we were captured by an enemy in our basic training, and although we were in Police Custody our young brains kicked into auto pilot and we refused all but basic information, except for what they could have gleaned from our wallets, and we refused to sign anything. The guards on the night had obviously had a long night and the last thing they wanted to deal with was 3 drunk soldiers, I saw that they were getting pissed off with us and the fat sweaty guard behind the counter smashed his baton on the countertop to remind us of who was boss, we just looked at each other and burst out laughing, we rolled around and kept laughing every time we made eye contact with each other, it was painful side splitting laughter, the type you can't stop. The guards had lost this round of the pissing competition and the main guard rolled his eyes back in his head and shrugged in defeat before leading 3 giggling soldiers off to their cells.

The fact we still had things like laces and belts was a bad omen and made me fear that the prisoners that were already there may also not have been searched properly. The guards from the night before didn't seem like the sharpest of characters, and they may have not searched the other prisoners too, this made it a possibility that the other prisoners had weapons that they had smuggled in, or a guard from the night before who had a grudge may have passed in a weapon to be used on us.

On stepping out of the shade of my cell and onto the dusty exercise yard I felt the heat of the day rising and I longed for a cold drink of water to quench my thirst, there was a tap in the toilet area but after one look at the unsanitary conditions within there I considered dehydration a better option. Leggy and Mad Willy were leant up against the wall near the guard post sipping water from chilled plastic water bottles, thankfully they had a third one for me.

"Morning wankers, what a fucking shit hole" was my cheerful opening,

We grinned at each other and discussed how much shit we were going to be in when we returned to camp, that was 'if' we returned to camp.

After only a few minutes I saw a large Greek guy coming out of one of the cells directly opposite to where we were stood, he paused at the gated entrance to his cell and scanned around like a general inspecting his army. He had a few humble greetings from the skinny wrecks that lay about in the shade and dust but he didn't respond as his gaze was now fixed on us!

This guy was huge, over 6ft tall and heavy built, not an athlete by a long shot, but big enough to throw a skinny 19 year old around like a rag doll. He was wearing a dirty white 'wife beater' vest and dirty jeans, he too looked like he had slept on the floor last night, funnily enough though he had no shoes on! Walking purposefully across the exercise yard this big bear of a man made a b-line for us; Mad Willy broke the silence,

"**Right, if this cunt starts we will all jump him!**"

It wasn't a request or an order, it was a statement of fact, this is what we would have to do! We would have swarmed around him like wasps and used our speed, aggression and with multiple small stings we would have attacked until he eventually gave up!

"**I'll bite his fucking ankles then shall I?**" I quipped.

As he neared I saw, although a big man, he was mostly fat, he had curly black hair, a sweaty olive skinned look about him and about 3 unshaven chins, this was going to be easier than I thought, we would have to just kept running him around until he dropped dead of a heart attack!

His large sweaty right hand shot forward with the palm open to offer a handshake,

"**You alright boys? Heard you boys come in last night, had a 'bit of bovva' yeah?**"

The biggest shock was his London accent and secondly was the big cheesy grin on his face,

"**Fucking hell mate I thought we were gonna have to fight you**" Leggy said in a relieved voice.

"**NAH NAH Mate, no one is gonna touch you in here, they heard what happened and think you are crazy bastards, they're just wankers, nothing to fear!**"

The big guy was called 'Kostas' and he asked us if we wanted breakfast, we did, and he appeared to have some influence within the jail because with a click of his fingers the sentry at the guard post was sent off to get us 3 breakfast sandwiches and some more water. What we didn't know was that in Jail in Cyprus at that time was that if you had no cash on you then you went hungry unless family bought food in for you, we had no money but Kostas didn't care about that it was small change to him. He explained that he had been caught on a speed boat in Larnaca bay trafficking thousands of Ecstasy tablets into the country for distribution to the night clubs across the whole of Cyprus.

"It was a fair cop, I was having engine problems and the coastguard just swooped in on me, I'll probably do some real time for it too"

Kostas appeared to be accepting of his fate, but he did give us a cheeky grin and said

"Unless I get bail, and some new shoes, then I'll do a runner back to London!"

in unison our band of Brits burst into laughter…

The laughter was short lived as 6 smartly dressed guards came to the gate and demanded that we exit the exercise yard! Looks like morning shift had started and they looked far more professional and capable than the slobs from the night before!

With 2 guards each we were soon placed in 'manacle' wrist and ankle restraints that were all joined together by chains and locked in place firmly. This type of 'chain gang' restraint stops you from being able to walk properly, never mind trying to run or escape. With a guard either side of each of us we were led back into the charge room where the mood was so much more professional and disciplined, we were presented to the officer behind the charge desk one by one. This guy looked like a right 'bastard' and had the air of authority about him that we were used to in the military, he was sharply dressed in a crisp ironed uniform and had tightly cropped hair that the Regimental Sergeant Major would have been proud of, he was not going to be taking any of our crap, and to be fair we were so hungover we were in no mood to give him any either. Our belts and laces were removed and bagged up with our wallets and we were sent back into the Exercise yard to await investigators who were waiting to interview us.

Kostas was waiting for us to return and he chuckled at the sight of us now holding up our cargo shorts as we no longer had belts,

"So, are you boys going to tell me what happened last night then? How did you end up in this mess?"

The day had begun like many before it, we always started work with PT at 6am, this was because it was cooler then and the Mediterranean sun was not belting out the full power of its heat, this made perfect sense in a hot country and ensured that soldiers didn't succumb to heat related injuries. However, like soldiers have done since soldiering was invented, we stayed out partying all night, with the afore mentioned Swedish ladies, in the local tourist hot spots, this also meant that we usually came in at half 5 in the morning from the bars of Ayia Napa or Larnaca still drunk! We dumped our going out clothes on the floor next to our beds and quickly changed into PT kit to start the day without a wink of sleep. So, the forethought of our cooler early morning fitness sessions was wasted, we were already dehydrated and exhausted from partying all night and were therefore not in the best of physical condition. PT was usually a 5-mile run or march in full combat gear, there were other beastings too along the way, just to fuck us about a bit more than usual. The Platoon Sergeant often found a nice hill along the route where we did shuttle runs up and down until we reached exhaustion and puked up the dregs of the booze we had been drinking just hours before. We showered and had breakfast after PT finished, then we worked through the morning either on the shooting range, being taught a class on field tactics, or like on most days, the limit of our leader's imagination went as far as vehicle maintenance or cleaning our accommodation until we had to finish work at 13:30pm. Afternoon's consisted of sleeping on the nearby beach and preparing our kit for the next day, we often started pre drinking with large bottles of local wine called 'Saint Panteleimon'; We aptly renamed it as 'Pandemonium', this sweet white wine was swigged from the bottle whilst we showered and ironed our going out clothes, its high alcohol content launched us into a super charged, hyperactive party mood which usually led to 'chaos and mayhem' in the bars of Larnaca or Ayia Napa.

Four of us set out for the night in a great mood, Leggy, Wiggy Mad Willy and myself wanted nothing more than a few drinks and to pick up some girls. We all thought we were the 'Bees Knees' because we were members of the 'Reconnaissance Platoon', also known as 'Recce Platoon', but pronounced 'REKKI'! The platoon was supposed to consist of the Battalions finest soldiers, they acted as forward observation teams just in front of and behind enemy lines, their role was to gather intelligence on the enemy and pass this information back to Battalion Command. Apparently we were the 'elite' of the Battalion! and having seen some of the soldiers in the rifle companies this was not a hard standard to reach, some of the platoons looked like a scene out of 'Zombie Apocalypse' with all there messed up faces and funny walks. Because of the 'elite' status put on us we were hated by the rest of the soldiers in Battalion; however, we were comfortable with that and wore it as a badge of honor which we used to taunt them with! The truth however, was that although we were mostly good at what we did, and were very keen soldiers, we were the biggest collection of misfits and chancers that you could have found, maybe these were the behaviors needed for the job at hand? Young mavericks, with an attitude, who were willing to take chances and go the extra mile to achieve their mission.

Leggy was the eldest in our group, he had been with 'Recce' in Northern Ireland where their surveillance skills were put to play against the IRA. He was a Battalion cricketer and was well known and popular. Leggy was a ladies' man and was a great 'Trapping Partner' who I bounced banter and chat up lines off when chatting up the girls in town, he was of course a real 'Poser' too who liked to not only look good in uniform but was always dressed like he was in a boy band when we went out.

Wiggy had come from 'A Company', the 'Bayonets', these were the Battalions first soldiers into battle and they always wore their

'Bayonets' with pride. He was a nice lad from Derbyshire who was also a poser and was obsessed with the most up to date military kit, he always had the latest gadget and would have spent his wages on the most bizarre things like torches that changed colour at the flick of a switch, a great idea if it didn't break the first time it was used. Wiggy was also a crack shot with a rifle and was part of both the Regimental and Army shooting team, he competed at Bisley and earnt the right to wear the badge of the Army's top 100 marksmen. Wiggy wasn't much of a party animal and often remained behind in camp when we went out, however, when he did come out he always got really drunk and was known to fall asleep or have uncontrollable fits of giggling.

'Mad Willy', like me, had come from 'B Company' after Northern Ireland, so I knew a bit about him, but he had been in a different platoon, so we had never really mixed. He had joined the Army after trying out as a deck hand on a fishing trawler in Cornwall, he hated every minute of it and decided to join the Army. Willy had received the nickname of 'Mad Willy' as people genuinely thought he was 'Mad', it was as simple as that. To the casual observer he was a grumpy man who hated authority, he had a penchant for knives and this unsettled people, especially when he sat at the end of his bed sharpening the blade whilst staring at them. However, if people had been bothered to dig deeper, as I did, then you would have found a person who had a dark sense of humor and only had respect for people who deserved it, he didn't suffer fools and didn't just hand out respect like confetti because someone was of a rank or a position of power.

At the stroke of Midnight we had queued with the other soldiers at the 'Popular Bank' cash point in Ayia Napa, for some reason the bank only allowed us to draw £60 a day from our bank accounts, maybe because they knew we would have blown our wages in a weekend had they not done it, or maybe it was a security protocol? So as problem-solving types, soldiers soon worked out that we were able to get another £60 out at just after midnight and continue partying. We headed back to the bright lights of the main square near the Mino's Bar where we joined the never-ending party scene, crowds of tourists drank cocktails and bounced in unison to the latest Scandinavian summer holiday music. We stood there slightly bouncing and doing our 'Squaddie Shuffle' dance, this was a type of dance that didn't need much movement or rhythm, we weren't the kids from 'Fame' and most of us had two left feet, we didn't care, we were just happy to be there in the moment, sipping our cold beers from the bottle and checking out the latest talent. At this time Ayia Napa was classed as one of the world's best party locations, it had the sun, the sea and the sex, and this was right at our doorstep, what more could have a 19 year old lad with a pocket full of cash want?

I'm not sure who suggested it, but it was time to move onto a night club where we aimed to drink until the early hours. There was no shortage of choice, but some were better than others, and if you went to some of the smaller places you were at risk of being the only British Soldier in there, at times that was a good thing, but at times not so good. Some of the local lads hated the competition we gave them with the ladies, we were paid better than them, we had better clothes, as we had more disposable cash, we were able to afford to buy girls drinks. The Swedish girls also liked us because we spoke better English than the Cypriot lads too, they obviously had never met members of our Pioneer Platoon, some of those guys were barely able to string together a sentence of understandable English! So, if a soldier was alone in a 'locals' club this was a potential flashpoint where they could have been jumped by a gang of Cypriot Youths who wanted to unleash some pent-up hatred they had for us.

We left the Main Square and headed back past the cashpoint where a queue of other drunken soldiers were lined up desperately waiting to withdraw the last dregs of their pitiful wages. We were heading for Pizazz Night Club on the edge of town, the night club owners used large beams of light which shot into the sky from spotlights, the lights were visible from miles around and it gave the effect of searchlights seeking out enemy bombers during the World War 2 'Blitz' of London. The powerful lights beamed into the clear night skies and danced around like heavenly strippers enticing clubbers into their party, it worked and we followed the light like moths to a bulb. As we continued along the road a metal extractor type outlet protruded from the side of a restaurant, it was made of thin square sheets of metal all pieced together to extract the cooking fumes from the kitchen area. It was also at the right height for drunken assholes, like us, to use as a large metallic drum; 'BOOM BUBBA BOOM BOOM, BAB BAB' sounded the large drum to our delight. However, we had not realized that at the opposite side of this extractor vent our drumming had sent piles of chimney ash crashing down on the food cooking beneath ruining it in the process. The angry 'chef' came storming out onto the street in a rage at us whilst brandishing a large cooking knife,

"YOU BLOODY BASTARDS, YOU RUIN MY FOOD" he raged,

We of course didn't care! We were drunk, selfish, aggressive teenagers who had no regard for anyone, let alone a local businessman who's profits for the night had just been covered in ash.

The 'chef' became more animated and started waving the blade around which just made us see 'red mist', we saw a threat and that turned us into vile animals who started taunting him to **'come and have a go, we will kill you with your own blade!'**

Chairs were thrown about at the front of the restaurant as the customers looked on in shock at what was unfolding in front of them!

Our attention then focused on a small red car sat outside on the street near to the Restaurant. In unison we gathered around it, and again I don't recall where the shout came from but I heard,

"LET'S ROLL HIS FUCKING CAR!"

Hands went around and under this small red car that had moments before just been sat there inanimate and causing no harm, we heaved at it from beneath the sills and with surprising ease and with a metallic bumper crunching crash the car rolled onto its roof!

We danced like Native Americans around a campfire whooping and continuing our barrage of threats towards the poor 'chef' who was just stood there looking stunned and dismayed at the shameful carnage we had created.

"THE POLICE ARE COMING", I heard a voice shout!

With the screams of madmen who were high on a mixture of adrenaline and booze we ran off towards the safety of the Night Club!…

First stop once in the Night Club, especially for me was the toilet, booze has always flown straight through me and tonight was no exception. As I returned to the darkened room that was booming with sounds of 90's club music, fake smoke and flashing disco lights I saw that my 3 partners in crime were surrounded by Police officers near to the entrance we had just come into. I should have walked away, swapped my top, crashed out through a fire exit and ran! Anything but what I did! I calmy walked over, Willy was shaking his head and mouthing at me to 'Fuck off', I took no notice, as with most drunk people, I thought I knew best, I wanted to sort this out diplomatically!

"What's going on here then, these boys have been in here with me for ages, they haven't done anything"

Greek words were spoken by the cops and I was bundled in with the other 3 and pushed outside the club. Once outside we escalated things again, although there were a few cops there were not enough to take us in if we didn't want to go! We refused to go in the Police van, we had heard there had been beatings dished out by the civilian police and didn't fancy any of that!

Wiggy saw his opportunity! Myself, Leggy and Willy were arguing with the cops about the van, Wiggy edged to one side and at the speed of a thousand gazelles he ran off along through the crowds of tourists that were now queueing to enter the club, Wiggy was never to be seen again, and had successfully made his escape from the clutches of the Cypriot Police. The Military Police soon arrived and coaxed us into their vehicles, we thought this may be our chance to be taken into military custody rather than Police custody. This however, was a short-lived dream and we were dropped off at Ayia Napa Police Station. The Cypriot Police appeared unwilling or unable to control us and we refused to go into any of the holding cells, we were convinced that they wanted us in there to give us a beating! We sat in the front waiting room where there was a TV for us to watch, we were locked in there but we still saw it as a victory. Later that night a white transport van fitted with cages arrived, we had been lulled into a false sense of security, at this point we lost control of our situation, Cypriot guards came in and we were handcuffed, our next destination was going to be the Police Jail in Larnaca! On route from Ayia Napa we had to drive past our camp at Dhekelia Garrison, I recall thinking that I had never longed to be in the safety of our barracks more than I did at that moment!

Kostas laughed at our tale of Pandemonium and the ensuing chaos and mayhem that occurred in the last few hours of our night out. His laughs were disturbed by the jingling of keys and the 'Clunk' of the jail gate being opened, we were summoned out and as we left the jail area I saw a British Army Land Rover painted in the distinctive sand and green colours we used for camouflage parked next to the charge desk entrance, this only meant one thing, the Military Police were here to take us away! It was a bittersweet feeling, on one hand I was getting out of this shit hole of a jail, but on the other hand I was now going to be in the clutches of the military discipline system and some of the meanest bastards that really knew how to punish us.

I looked back and waved at Kostas who still had a big cheerful grin on his face, he returned the wave and sauntered back to the other degenerates that littered the cells, master of his kingdom and as happy as a pig in shit!

The Military Police who arrived were actually our own Regimental Provost Police, these were the nasty bastards that kept discipline tight in camp and made your life hell with physical beastings or what were called show parades, these were used to get a grip of sloppy uniforms or minor discipline infringements, a Corporal or a Sergeant would have ripped you a new asshole for the breach of standards and then award you a 6pm and 10pm inspection at the Guard Room! This messed up your evening and you knew that if you failed the inspection that you would have been back the next night for a dose of the same until you passed the standards set by the individual Provost Corporal. If you were really unlucky, and I was, you would have been awarded 'Restriction of privileges!' also known as 'Rippers', this was awarded by the Company or Battalion Commanders for more serious breaches of discipline and was just one stage short of being placed in Regimental Jail. 'Rippers' consisted of parading at 5am in PT kit so you were able to join your platoon afterwards for PT, another parade at 1pm where you would have been worked hard in the sun picking up litter or keeping the Guardroom clean, then at 6pm and 10pm you would have again paraded with the 'show parades', and then as an added bonus you had to parade again at Midnight. This really did mess your life up; 7 days jail was considered easier than 7 days 'Rippers' because you didn't do the day-to-day stuff with your own platoon on top of the punishments.

The Provost Corporal went quite easy on us, we had been bailed to return for a decision to be made on what was going to happen to us, so there was not much he could do, we had actually not been found guilty of any crime. However, the Adjutant of the Battalion, who oversaw discipline, had decreed that we were to be gated pending an outcome, this basically meant we were not allowed to leave the camp, like being under house arrest, but in a big house with about 650 soldiers in, and a bar… The Adjutant was a great bloke really, he was fondly known as 'Tommo' by the troops, he had a mess of blonde floppy hair and spoke with an upper-class accent that would have put the Royal Family to shame, a proper toff! But he had a soft spot for us, he knew we were good soldiers and just lads growing up, he called us 'Little Scoundrels' in a cheeky rogue's kind of way that showed he empathised with our situation.

We were trained Soldiers, trained to fight and kill! It was foolish to think that when off duty we were going to be boy scouts, there must be a chapter in a training manual somewhere that teaches this to Officers and Senior Ranks because at that time there were a lot of Soldiers getting into trouble for similar things! The Battalion had just finished an intensive 2 year tour of Northern Ireland and the troops were letting off steam! I believe the modern Military terminology is 'Decompressing', except we didn't get any offers of counselling or activities to divert our aggression, we were left to sort it out for ourselves. The sad fact was that we lost more Soldiers in Cyprus to drink driving and mental health related incidents than we had in the past 2 years of fighting the IRA! What did they expect to happen? 'Here you go boys, unlimited alcohol and parties', this was the reward for us, but it was the wrong reward! Cyprus could have been so much better, we were young men who had no direction and yearned to be treated as professional soldiers, most of the time though we were treated like crap and no better than conscripts.

Although the Adjutant had gated us, it was a token effort to show that he had tried to do something, it was impractical, and they had no way of enforcing it either, within 24 hours we had snuck out of camp and headed back to the bright lights of Ayia Napa! 'Mad Willy' was smuggled out in the back of a car and Leggy and I snuck out in a large group of the lads who had hidden us between them, the Party was back on! Later that night though our escape and evasion to Ayia Napa was discovered; 'Tommo', and a young Sub Lieutenant, who shall remain nameless, were out on the town and came across us in the main town square. 'Tommo' grabbed me from behind and instinctively I threw him over my shoulder, I looked down to see the Adjutant laying on the floor, he was shocked, dazed and a bit drunk too, 'Tommo' brushed it off as a hilarious situation and insisted that we stayed the rest of the night with him, that way he could make sure we stayed out of trouble, he even bought the beers!

A few weeks later we returned to the Police Station to find that they were not going to charge us with anything. 'Tommo' had worked his magic, and like the smooth-talking lounge lizard he was, he had made an agreement with the owner of the car that we were to pay for the damage we had caused and he wouldn't press charges. Had he not done this we could have faced real jail time, it was good to know that he was looking out for us, a true Officer and a Gentleman!

Wiggy's escape from the Cypriot Police had become a tale of legends around the Battalion, he was the one that got away whilst we were the ones that got caught, troops can forgive anything, as long as you don't get caught! However, Wiggy's escape wasn't as easy as just running away; Wiggy was, as I have said before, not the best of drinkers, he ran like the wind and made enough distance to hide somewhere in case more Police were on route to conduct a search. On seeing an advertising billboard Wiggy in drunken exhaustion jumped through the foliage and brush with the intention of hiding behind the billboard until the dust settled. Unbeknown to Wiggy though there was a shear drop behind the billboard into which he fell. As he landed abruptly he banged his head and knocked himself out, after a few minutes of lying unconscious on the rocky ground Wiggy began to stir, his head was pounding and he felt an uneasy sickness like a hangover. After staggering to his feet and brushing himself down Wiggy strolled back towards the scene of our crime, he had to go past it to get to the taxis in the town and complete his escape. The car was still on its roof and the Police were trying in desperation to control the scene, party goers were milling around and there was no control over access to the vehicle; Wiggy, being a master escape artist also had the forethought of forensic evidence, he mixed in with the crowd and began wiping our hand prints off the car with his T shirt, clever lad. One of the cops saw him and moved towards him and began shouting at him to stop where he was. Fearing arrest Wiggy did what Wiggy was good at… he ran… he was, 'The One That Got Away!'

AWOL

(Absent Without Leave)

It was a dark windy night, but it was also hot on the tarmac of the runway which was radiating the heat it had stored from being baked in the sun all day. We crouched down in rows known as 'sticks', the runway lights were off, and the tower and surrounding buildings had also joined us in the darkness as we awaited our covert extraction from the island's main runway at Akrotiri airbase in Cyprus. In the distance I saw the twinkling lights of Limassol and the wind blew off the sea cooling us, part of me wished I were in the clubs of Limassol, but I needed a break from the destructive camp and clubbing routine that I had gotten used to, also the soldier in me loved the anticipation of the adventure on which we were about to embark.

In the distance I heard the distinctive deep buzz of the C130 Hercules transporter aircraft as they approached, these were specially adapted aircraft that were flown just above sea level by American Special Forces Pilots who were using night vision goggles and aircraft instruments instead of runway lights to land the aircraft, this was standard procedure for extracting troops under the cover of darkness in hostile environments. The transporter flights charged in at a belly hugging height and I flinched involuntarily as the landing gear screeched into the tarmac runway next to me, I felt the heat from the propellers as they passed and I was hit by the strong acrid smell from the backblast of aviation fuel as the aircraft taxied ahead, the engines maintained full revs as we loaded the aircraft to ensure we had a quick takeoff. The 'sticks' of troops that formed our Reconnaissance Platoon embarked onto the aircraft and I was soon secure in my hammock seat, the seats ran the length of the aircraft and I was strapped in with a canvas roll pin belt for safety, all heavy equipment had been placed into cargo nets on the deck, this left us with our rifles, webbing and helmets. The engines roared into life and the aircraft jerked forward as we sped down the runway for a covert extraction out into the darkness of the Mediterranean Sea. The C130's remained just above sea level for around 30 minutes, just low enough to avoid detection by the islands radar system, once we were safe from detection we rose up to a cruising height and headed towards Germany.

'Panzer Kaserne' is situated in Southern Germany in a town called Boblingen on the outskirts of Stuttgart, Field Marshall Erwin Rommel was Commandant there during World War 2 and the camp still had the air of that period about it. The large 3 story barrack blocks had a traditional and functional feel about them with their sharp white exteriors and steep grey tiled roofs, the cobbled roads were wide and very obviously built to take the weight and destructive power of the World War 2 armored 'Panzer tanks', all that was missing from this scene was long red flags draped from the buildings with the black and white 'Swastika' insignia of the Nazi's. After the defeat of Germany in World War 2 many of the German bases were taken over as part of the occupation, this prevented the reemergence of the Nazi's, but it was also to stop the Red Army from expanding further into Germany when the 'Cold War' began. Panzer Kaserne was now occupied by 'The 10th Special Forces Group (Airborne), 1st Special Forces! We were to be enrolled onto a 3-week briefing and training schedule where we were to learn the skills they used in various operations, these included Long Range Reconnaissance, explosives, survival skills and weapons systems used by Russian and American forces. The United States Special Forces or 'Green Berets' have a long history of training soldiers across the world, their motto is 'DE OPPRESSO LIBER', translated this means 'To Free from Oppression' or 'To Liberate the Oppressed'. Part of the role of the 'Green Berets' is to infiltrate into war zones with the aim of training and arming 'Guerilla' forces, these soldiers can be men and women from a downtrodden community who have suffered at the hands of a tyrannical war lord or a nation rebuilding in the image of democracy, these soldiers are usually trained to fight a superior force. The mystique of the 'Green Berets' has been show cased in TV shows like 'The A Team' and on the big screen with John Wayne's Vietnam war film, which was imaginatively titled, 'The Green Berets', and further interest in the 'Green Berets' was generated with Sylvester Stallone's series of 'Rambo' films.

As with any military training experience things always start with fitness, it's the basis of all things military, if you are not fit enough to deal with the harshness of the battlefield then you are of little use as a Soldier, you will fall behind and soon become a casualty of war that will need to be looked after, this in turn adds a lot of demand on medical resources.

The day started with morning 'formation'; this was when the whole unit paraded on the main square for morning PT. Most of the Americans had the standard grey t shirts with 'ARMY' printed across the front, some had a mixture of other sportswear, we however were smartly dressed in our 'RECCE' t shirts and black shorts, compared to our hosts we looked like Guardsman on parade outside Buckingham palace! Once 'formation' was complete we were introduced to our training team; Rambo, john Wayne and the A Team they were not! A common mistake when people think about 'Special Forces' is that they think they are all Supermen who bristle with muscles and can run for miles without stopping, it's not true, they are usually very motivated and clever people who achieve extraordinary things, but they are ultimately just people.

The training team were all in the thirties and forties by the look of them, they were carrying some body weight and wore ill-fitting sportwear that was probably purchased in their younger years. Most of us were barely twenty and didn't even know what body fat was, but we were sure that these guys were going to put us through our paces.

The Gunnery Sergeant stepped forward to address us,

"OK GUYS, TODAY WE ARE GOING TO START WITH OUR BASIC FITNESS TEST, WE RUN FOR A MILE AN A HALF IN YOUR OWN TIME, THERE IS A SAFETY WAGON, JUST FOLLOW THAT AND Y'ALL BE FINE."

We walked down to the start point and lined up across the road, the safety vehicle began to pull away and the order to 'GO!' was barked out! Fitness tests like this were nothing new to us and it showed immediately! The Platoon surged ahead leaving our new training team in our wake with a cloud of dust for them to chew on. The pace increased as 30 young lions roared ahead attempting to gain a personal best time to beat the others in the Platoon, it was a competitive environment, and we were always pushed to over deliver and to push each other further. Due to this competitive nature we had some very fit team members who had the most unbelievable capacity for running at speed, I was not one of these people, in my early years as a soldier I struggled to keep with the pack, however, others leapt forward with such speed they soon caught up with the safety vehicle which was chugging along at a pace to remain in sight, 'Al stone', one of our best runners was soon up next to the driver's door urging him to speed up, Al had become the pacer, and I suppose by default the safety vehicle!

At the end of the test run we were soon rejoined by our 'special forces mentors who were coughing up phlegm and spitting out chewing tobacco like only an American can do;

"GOD DAMN IT BOYS, I THOUGHT YOU WERE GUNNA KICK HOLES IN THE SAFETY WAGON!"

The second part of the mornings PT consisted of a gentle leg stretch through the local forest, unfortunately for our American hosts we set the pace! After a second dose of British Army Fitness, it was announced that all future runs were to be taken by one of the American soldiers in camp who was a seasoned marathon runner, our training team had decided to meet up with us afterwards and leave the morning fitness sessions to their 'Running Guy'. These were 'Special Forces' and knew which battles to fight, being physically destroyed by young infantryman was not a battle worth fighting!

We soon settled into camp life at 'Panzer Kaserne', the Americans had added a few home comforts in the way that only Americans can; There was a bowling alley, fast food joint and a few bars dotted around the camp which catered for the various American cultures like the 'Rod and Gun' for the 'Rednecks', the bar actually had a gun shop in it! Another one of the bars in a nearby camp was almost exclusively for African Americans where they listened to up to date 'Rap' or 'Motown and Blues', I'm not sure if they had a gun shop but you most definitely smelt the Cannabis. Each day we started with PT and then we had various training modules to complete, it was great to be learning new skills from some of the best soldiers in the world and I dreaded the thought of returning to the routine of normal Battalion life.

As quick as the training started it stopped, the camp became a ghost town! President BUSH had ordered American troops into Somalia to support the humanitarian mission that was failing in the country at that time. The Special Forces were put on standby to deploy to Somalia where their skills in Surveillance, and their ability to safely extract downed Pilots would have been of great benefit if things started going wrong when the forces moved in. We had now become guests with no purpose, our training teams were sent to their operational commands so no training took place, the cookhouse was closed and as a get by they issued us with ration packs known as MRE's, or 'Meals Ready to Eat', these were tasteless packs of ambient food which could have been eaten hot or cold, they were soon discarded and renamed 'Meals Rejected by the English'. Then the inevitable happened, we got bored! Too much spare time had the predictable result of an exodus of troops into the bright lights of Stuttgart. We gravitated to the cheap bars, brothels and strip joints that are quite common in German life, for an Englishman it is a totally alien experience to sit in what on the surface looks like a normal pub and enjoy a beer whilst pornographic videos are played on loop and pregnant strippers get whipped on a stage at the far end of the bar, but in Germany it is quite accepted that most towns and Cities have a 'Red light District', so when in Rome… I was the only one of our group that spoke any German, so I was nominated as interpreter with the arduous task of ordering 'FUNF FLASHE BEER BITTER', that's 'five bottles of beer please', or 'WELCHE KOSTEN', that roughly translates to 'what cost?', that was usually reserved for the pregnant strippers.

Thankfully before we were relieved of all our wages the American forces had deployed into Somalia without the need for our hosts, training recommenced, and we deployed onto our final Long Range Reconnaissance exercise. Our 4-man team was led by Rob SCOTT, he was a Colour Sergeant and a very experienced soldier too, as an added bonus he was a really nice chilled out guy who had nothing to prove to anyone and that made for a good leader. Rob was new to the Platoon and had been stitched up by the other Team Commanders, they had put the teams together before he came and he was dumped with 3 reprobates that the other teams didn't really want, we were trouble and weren't part of their cliques either, so Rob was lumbered with us. Baz Mitchell was a young Lance Corporal at the time and had a reputation as a hardened street fighter from Nottingham, this was a good thing as it kept Myself and Mad Willy in check, we weren't going to answer back or slack off because if we did there was a good chance that Baz would have broken our jaws with his infamous right hook. We liked Baz too and respected him as a soldier so behaving wasn't going to be a problem for me and Mad Willy, putting us together as a team actually worked out well and we consistently performed well in competitive events against the other so called 'elite' teams. I think that knowing they wanted us to fail gave us more drive to succeed and be able to say, 'Fuck You!'

The initial briefing was given by our 'Umpire', he was a 'Special Forces Ranger', and his job was to give us the locations of our tasks and to advise us in what actions to take and how the US forces would conduct their patrols. He would remain with us in the shadows for the next few days and de-brief us after each task had been completed. The aim of the first patrol was to locate a military communications base, once we had located it, we were to complete a Close Target Reconnaissance (CTR), We were to observe our target and report back information that would have been of use to an attacking force. As our information was time critical we moved at speed, however, moving tactically at speed across wild terrain is easier said than done whilst carrying enough ammunition, water, food and equipment for 4 days in our 'Bergan's'. The 'Bergan' is a military term for a large rucksack, it is the bane of all Infantrymen, this large pack is filled with the essentials that a soldier will need to survive for long periods of time in the field. You pack it with a sleeping system, a shelter, food, water, spare clothing, radio batteries, ammunition, mortar bombs. Basically, if it needs carrying it goes in the 'Bergan', which then goes on the back of the soldier, who then has to carry a ridiculous amount of weight strapped up high on their back. Soldiers are often lifted by their arms just to be able to stand up due to the weight, this was definitely going to be a test of our navigational skills, fieldcraft and our physical endurance!

We strapped our 'Bergan's' to our backs and set off at pace into the deep Bavarian forests of South Germany, these ancient forests are the places where ancient folk tales of Werewolves and fairy tale castles came from. Castles with steep white towers on rock escarpments shot out of the tree canopy like a magical scene from a Disney film, to add to this magical scene superstitious locals had planted large white crosses on hillsides to ward off evil spirits and Werewolves from the forest, it made for one of the most breath taking and beautiful scenes I have ever seen.

Dusk was setting in and the forest became damp and cold, a mist had developed that lay across the forest floor like smoke from a campfire, this gave the ground under the tree canopy a haunted feeling that made you understand why the locals felt that the woods were inhabited by spirits that may do them harm. Carrying our heavy 'Bergan's' we moved tactically as possible through the trees, we were near to our target and needed a 'forming up point'(FUP) and 'emergency rendezvous point' (ERV). We stopped about 500m short of the target, it was a dip in the ground that had a large boulder next to it which made it identifiable in the dark, this would have been where we dropped the heavy equipment and have a final brief before we moved out to complete the CTR. Our brief was quick and simple, we didn't need in depth orders as we knew what our roles and responsibilities were. The plan was for 2 teams to probe the outer defences of the position and take note of the relevant intelligence, we used a clover leaf pattern of probing, moving in and out of the target in a clockwise rotation, this made a route outline shaped like that of a clover leaf, allowing for a 360-degree view of the position. Rob and Mad Willy maintained cover from a 'friendly fire location', we knew where they would be and they covered Baz and I as we were moving in for the Preliminary CTR, if things went wrong, their job was to lay down suppressing fire whilst we escaped back to the ERV.

A sentry was posted and we checked each other over for noisy kit that may rattle or shine, we didn't want the slightest noise to give us away, we added more camouflage cream to each other's faces too as what we had put on earlier had been sweated off during the march in. The basics of camouflage and concealment were our biggest defence to compromise, so we took our time and checked them off.

- Shape, we added foliage to our equipment to break up the distinctive shape of a man, and to break up any of the straight lines on our rifles.
- Shine, we ensured that there were no shiny surfaces, including our faces, exposed.
- Shadow, in lighter conditions we may have cast shadows that may be seen as we hid behind buildings or trees.
- Silhouette, when we moved, we avoided the skyline.
- Spacing, in nature there are no regular patterns so whilst patrolling we moved at irregular distances between each other.
- Sudden movement, all movement had to be slow and purposeful, no waving of arms or rushing around, this would have drawn the attention of any half decent sentry.
- Aircraft, be aware of patterns left on the ground by movement that can be seen from above, also looking up at aircraft can expose skin on the neck that hasn't been covered in camouflage cream.

Weapons and ammunition were checked and prepared, but they were only there as a last resort, we were here for information, not a fight.

Our 4-man team drifted out of the 'ERV' like ghosts, from here forward our only communication with each other was with hand signals, we were soft underfoot and moved with stealth whilst observing our arcs with our rifle butts in the shoulders at the 'ready'. In turn we all looked back at our 'ERV' to ensure that we knew what it looked like from this angle, this made it easier to find if we had to make a quick extraction under fire! We had rehearsed this 'CONTACT' drill many times, the 'lead scout' laid down a burst of fire and then 'peeled back' behind the next man who did the same, then the next, and this was repeated and it always ensured that any movement backwards was covered by fire, this 'peeling off' maneuver would continue until we 'broke contact' and made our way back to the 'ERV', where we regrouped, carried out ammunition and casualty checks, and then 'Bugged Out' with all of our equipment.

We stopped just short of the target, I heard the sounds of people milling around the base, generators were running and there was also a campfire that lit up the forest clearing, Rob and Mad willy broke off to their cover position and myself and Baz moved forward…

The type of information we were looking for was,

- Safe routes in and out.
- Enemy strength.
- Type of enemy, are they special forces or conscripts?
- Defenses and guard routines.
- Weapons.
- Vehicles.
- Supply, are they well fed and equipped? Is their morale good?
- Third party risks like a close by civilian population.
- Communications, do our radios work there?
- A sketch map of the layout of the camp, a picture paints a thousand words.

The list can be endless, and every piece of information gleaned is a valuable asset to the commander who planned the eventual attack on the position.

'**Crack!**'… I heard the sound to my left and slowly turned my head to see a sentry walking through the brush towards us. He hadn't seen us, he was walking a circular patrol route that looped the base, he came closer until he paused about 5 metres away. The Soldier wore an American woodland camouflage uniform with a peaked baseball style cap on his head, he slung his Armalite Rifle across his right shoulder and sparked up a cigarette which lit up his face as he drew deeply inhaling a lung full of smoke. I considered grabbing him from behind in a classic sentry takedown with my hand over his mouth and my foot in the back of his knees, we could have taken him as a prisoner and extracted intelligence from him! The sentry was a big lad but between Baz and myself I was sure we could have done it, it was a fleeting thought, a stupid one, if we had taken him we would have made too much noise, he would have put up a fight, and even if we had got away with it we would have alerted the enemy that something was wrong when they realised a sentry was missing. I snatched myself away from these thoughts,

'Just lye still and observe, he will fuck off soon and we can get on with the CTR.'

Soon enough the sentry moved on and we began our circular probe of the base, once we had completed the 'clover leaf' and gained a detailed plan of the base we rejoined Rob and Mad Willy and moved back to the ERV. We sat still in the darkness and listened in ambush positions in case we had been followed, once we were satisfied it was safe we shared the information about the base between us, that way if any of us were killed on route out there would have been a better chance of the shared intelligence surviving.

Once we were clear the 'umpire' that had been shadowing us gave Rob our next objective, this process was to be repeated over and over for the rest of the exercise causing us to crisscross miles of dense forest to locate our next objectives. The long marches took their toll on our bodies and we all had sore and blistered feet, some of the other teams had to seek medical aid and were unable to finish as a complete team, all of the Soldiers who succumbed to injuries were good soldiers to a man! But the fact that our team of unwanted reprobates finished as a complete unit did bring a smile to our faces, and it was a definite 'fuck you' moment!

'Endex' was called, and our tired and blistered bodies were loaded onto large 'Deuce and half' American Army Lorries, we travelled back to 'Panzer Kaserne' where we feasted on hot food from the cookhouse and stripped and cleaned our Weapons and bodies. It was nearly time to head back to Cyprus, there was only one thing to do, grab a weekend of Rest and Relaxation and maybe get drunk!

German bars are great, they have character, and the beer is always good, the bar staff take pride in their presentation and that of the beer, like an artist with a brush they skim the head off the top of a long glass of freshly poured brew which they bring to your table with swift efficiency. Myself and Mad Willy found our way to such an establishment and began sinking glass after glass of strong German Beer from long boot shaped glasses, a few shots were thrown in by the barman who was keen for us to stay and drink. Conversation between us had mostly been about our impending return to camp life in Cyprus, we both hated it and dreaded the prospect, the past 3 weeks had been great and we didn't want it to end, we loved being soldiers but felt that back at Battalion too much time was given over to being idle. We spoke about conflicts around the world and wondered how we could have got involved in some real action, some trigger time perhaps. The war in the Former Yugoslavia was still ongoing and they were taking foreign volunteers, that was just a train journey east from here, there was also the Foreign Legion, they had a savage reputation for brutality and hard training, that was what we wanted!

VIVE LA LÉGION

A mixture of fatigue and copious amounts of German beer and spirits took effect, Mad Willy started getting grumpy and aggressive and we fell out, the barman had now had enough of the foul-mouthed Brits and ejected us from the bar onto the street. After a bit of pushing and shoving in the street I walked off leaving Mad Willy who had now turned his anger to a passing car that had nearly run him over, I saw him swing his right foot at the rear light cluster of a BMW, he missed his target and fell to the floor in a heap. I walked off, I was drunk but aware enough to know to keep away from Willy when he was like that, he was violent and unpredictable, I wasn't going to stick around for that!

By the time I had got back to camp I was blind drunk and hell bent on joining the Foreign Legion, all I had to do was head West and cross the border into France, the dye was cast and a drunk decision was made! I threw some essentials into my 'Bergan'; a sleeping bag, rations and change of clothes, I wouldn't need much, but I thought I needed to take enough to spend at least 2 nights under the stars. I staggered out of the camp gates and headed off into the night, I used my compass to find west and picked the first main road I found that ran in that direction.

Hitch hiking wasn't a new thing to me, I had done it for many years, and it was probably the most cost-effective way of getting around. It didn't take long until my first lift came along, the driver of the car, an old guy called 'Henry', I suspected he was as drunk as me, he spoke good English and I told him I was going to France to join the Legion. He was ecstatic with excitement and wanted to help me with my adventure,

"YOU CAN STAY AT MY PLACE TONIGHT, AND IN THE MORNING WE WILL SEND YOU ON YOUR WAY!"

It was nearly midnight by now and I was starting to flag a bit, so I accepted his kind offer.

The next day I woke up on a sofa in a car repair garage, The sofa was an old musty smelling thing in a workshop area that the staff obviously used for their tea breaks. The place smelt of diesel and oil and light shone in through clear plastic corrugated roof panels, the air was filled with the clattering and whizzing noises of people at work on cars. Looking up from my slumber I saw

'Henry', he was there to greet me with a much-needed steaming hot cup of tea and a plate of toast, German hospitality at its finest I thought.

"So, Englishman, are you going to France today"

"Yes mate, I need to find my way though. Have you got a map?"

'Henry' thought for a second and walked off into a small office in the corner, when he returned he presented me with photocopies of a road map showing me the route to the nearest border crossing at 'Strasbourg' which was situated on the River Rhine. To get there I would have to cross through the 'Black Forest', I was now glad that I had packed a few essentials for the journey and worn walking boots. I was still a bit drunk so I still thought this expedition was a good idea, I packed away my sleeping bag and prepared to head off west, but before I was able to leave 'Henry' came running over with a bag of supplies for me, he was still excited about my 'Big adventure' and had emptied the cupboards in the factory kitchen, we filled up my 'Bergan' with tins of beans and beef stew and I thanked him for his hospitality. I waved him farewell as I headed off, some of the guys from the workshop came out and waved and cheered as I left too, they obviously wanted to see the 'Crazy Englishman' going off on his adventures, or maybe deep down they too wished they were young and stupid enough to pack a bag and leave their lives behind too.

It wasn't long until I was deep in the 'Black Forest', it is an amazing place with steep wooded hills and crystal-clear rivers, there were good roads too and I had no problem hitch hiking my way through, everyone I met knew some English and all were kind and generous to me, I was a young fresh faced looking guy, so I doubt that anyone saw me as a threat. By early evening I had reached the charming town of 'Oppenau', a river cascaded through its center and the hillsides that flanked the valley were lush with rich forests from which streams cascaded down to join the river, I never knew places like this existed, it was relaxing, I was strangely at peace with myself. I paused here for a while taking in the view and I ate some of beef stew and beans that 'Henry' had given me whilst I plotted my route on the photocopied road map, I didn't have far to go, and I was confident that I would have soon got a lift to the border.

My thumb wasn't out for long and I was at the border within a couple hours, the dark of the night had set in and the forests were now behind me as I entered the industrial border towns of the Rhine. A kind driver had taken me out of his way and to the river bridge that led over the Rhine from 'Kehl' to the French city of 'Strasbourg', the bridge ahead was a long well-lit road bridge with a path for pedestrians, it was adorned with both French and German flags in a show of European unity, there was a small *Tabac'* shop on the German side that sold tobacco, newspapers and postcards, the French customs post was in the distance on the far side. This was now becoming a reality and I may not have been able to contact anyone for a while, so I used the last of my cash to buy a postcard and a stamp and penned together a quick message to let my parents know where I was, there was no point in them being worried about me. It then dawned on me that I was going to need my passport to cross into France, I feared the worst and after checking through my bag I realized that in my drunken haste I hadn't packed it, it was still in camp back at 'Panzer Kaserne!' 'Fuck, Fuck, Fuck!' Can I join the Legion with no passport? How was I going to cross into France? I could have possibly swum across the Rhine and used my Bergan as a floatation pack? That was an extreme solution and looking off the bridge at the river I doubt I would have made it across, the cold water would have sapped my energy or one of the many barges that were chugging up and down would have run me over. I would have to front it out and see if I was able to bluff my way through the customs post on the French side by just walking through! I strapped my 'Bergan' onto my back and headed off across the bridge, 'just look ahead, don't make eye contact and keep walking', confidence and the ability to look like you belong somewhere can get you through a lot of situations, if you look 'furtive' and 'suspicious' then you draw attention to yourself, 'just look ahead, don't make eye contact and keep walking!'

As I approached the French Customs post I saw that there was only one guard on duty, he was in an office that looked out over the bridge through a large Perspex window, I looked into the office and I saw that he was reading a paper and glanced up every so often at the TV which was situated on the far side of his desk, there was a window with a sliding window which faced the pathway, this was where Passports of Identification documents would have been checked, this was closed and the guard seemed disinterested as I approached, 'just look ahead, don't make eye contact and keep walking!'

'Just look ahead, don't make eye contact and keep walking!'

'Just look ahead, don't make eye contact and keep walking!'

I was through, my nerve had held and my confidence had got me into France, I felt like a World War 2 Prisoner of War who had escaped the Nazi's! The guard hadn't even looked up to wave me through, at the time I thought this was quite an achievement, but years on I now look back in amusement because Europe had had open borders since the 1985 Schengen Agreement, they hadn't been stopping people for 7 years, for me though, at that time, and as a Soldier who had gone Absent Without Leave (AWOL), it was quite a gut-wrenching experience.

In broken French I found my way to the Police Station **"Ou est le poste de Police?"**, my pronunciation must have been a bit off and my ability to understand the replies was also a bit off… but I got there. I had read that the Police Stations in France will arrange transport to the Legion recruiting centers, so I presented myself at the desk and asked the Police Officer on the desk for some help **"excusez-moir monsieur Ou est la Legion Entrangere? Je suis anglaise, Je ne parle pas Francais"** that was it, I had no more

HARD STOP

French to give, not bad for a self-taught man but far from enough to survive on. The Police Officer looked up at me and walked over to a draw, he took out a piece of A4 paper and drew a map on it, the map showed a route to the Legion Recruiting Center which was situated only a few streets away, I thanked him for his time and not for the first time in the past 24hrs I slung my 'Bergan' on my back and headed off into the night. The map was simple to follow and I soon found myself on the edge of town walking down a deserted road, the map ended here so I must be near, then I saw a man walking towards me, he was dressed in the uniform of a Foreign Legion Soldier, he had a Black 'Kepi' hat on, Legionnaires usually wear a white 'Kepi' this meant he was a Sergeant or higher in rank. As he got nearer I saw that he was unsteady on his feet and looked scruffy and disheveled, this guy was 'shit faced drunk', I stopped him and asked the way to the Recruiting center, he just stared at me in disbelief, I asked again, he just stared at me… I was just about to walk away when he pointed to the white wall on the side of the pavement I had just walked along, I stood back and looked back the way I had come, along the whole length of the wall ran thick black painted letters bigger than me that spelled out **'LEGION ENTRANGERE'** I was a bit embarrassed that I hadn't seen this and the soldier belly laughed at me and slapped me on the shoulder when he saw my realization. The wall was actually part of an Army barracks so I followed it to the front entrance where two Soldiers stood guard, one looked like a regular French soldier and the other was a Legionnaire, The Legionnaire greeted me like a friend and led me inside to the *'Caporal'* who was sat behind a desk in his office, the *'Caporal'* looked like a seasoned soldier, he was lean and fit looking, like you would expect from a Legionnaire, his dark Mediterranean olive skin and bald head reminded me of a chocolate 'Malteser', in my regiment he would have definitely been known by the nick name 'Malteser Head'! Inside the barracks was like many military bases I had been in before, long polished corridors with dormitories and washrooms branching off from them. I saw some of the new recruits milling around in their green boiler suits, they looked happy, and the place felt safe after being outside on the cold streets of the city. There was a kitchen too, and being a French establishment, I could smell it, the sounds of cutlery clinking and smells of garlic and fresh bread were making me feel hungry. The *'Caporal'* behind the desk asked me for my Passport, I explained that I didn't have it, he asked for ID, so I passed him the only ID I had which was my British Army identification, he seemed happy with this, and he led me into a TV room to wait. The TV was playing a Legion recruiting video in German and 3 young lads were sat in there watching it, two of the three had bruises all over their faces and their clothes looked battered like they had been fighting, what were they running from? The Foreign Legion has a long history of taking soldiers from all over the world into their ranks. Young adventurers, romantics and runaways hiding from all manner of woes came here trying to start a new life, they travelled across the world to fight for France, and in return they can be given a new identity and French Citizenship, all that France asks is 5 year's military service. You don't have to change your name if you don't want to, and you don't have to have citizenship, it is just there as an option for those that need it, looking at the state of the three Germans, I guessed they were going to have new French sounding names very soon.

After about 30 minutes the Corporal returned, he had my ID with him,

"No, you must have passport, you go and come back with passport!"

I was gutted, but I knew he was right, the legion was part of a NATO country, they couldn't take AWOL soldiers from other NATO countries, this would have caused them too much political grief, I was shown the door and let out into the cold of the night. My whole Foreign Legion experience had lasted less than an hour, what was I going to do now? There was no point in dwelling on it,

I needed to make a plan! Option 1, I could have hitch hiked east to the Former Yugoslavia and volunteer there as a mercenary, the war there was in full swing and fighters from all over the world were heading there to join military units. This didn't feel right though, I had heard about the genocide of civilians over there and didn't fancy being expected to kill innocent people for a cause I didn't even understand. Option 2, head into North Germany and hand myself into a British Army base, but that would have only meant a quick journey to an Army jail in an unknown regiment until I was transported back to Cyprus, that could have spelled some hard jail time as I had no allies there, this would have caused a lot of unnecessary grief for the Army too who would have to administer my transportation… Or Option 3, make best speed and get back to 'Panzer Kaserne' where I would have to take my punishment from my own unit, I knew how they worked and had allies on the provost staff that would have looked after me. It had taken me less than 16 hours to cross Germany to France and my unit were not flying back to Cyprus for another 48 hours, it was a no brainer, if I moved fast, I'd make it back in time, what's the worst they could have done to me, put me in jail for 7 days, bring it on!!!

It was late now, I had been on the move now for nearly 24hrs, I had hitch hiked 150km from Stuttgart in Germany to Strasbourg in France, my feet ached and my shoulders were hurting from the weight of my 'Bergan', it was time to sleep. I crossed back over to the German side of the border with the intention of finding somewhere to sleep near the river, I soon found out that this was a bad idea, the land around the Rhine was swampy and not suitable, thank God I hadn't tried a river crossing, I would have most definitely got stuck in the swampy banks and drowned in the mud. I walked a little further out and soon found myself in an industrial area of 'Kehl', it was a rundown area and appeared to be a magnet for young Turkish looking guys who were just milling around on street corners. This triggered my survival instincts immediately, the hairs on the back of my neck stood up and I sensed danger! Here I was a young 20-year-old lad walking alone with a 'Bergan' on my back, I was wearing a green fleece jacket, blue jeans and had walking boots on too, I stood out as a tourist, maybe a backpacker crossing Europe, this made me a target of a potential 'Robbery'! Luckily when I had packed my 'Bergan' back at 'Panzer Kaserne' I had also packed a Combat Knife, it was my favorite one, an American M5 bayonet, it was robust and made for hand to hand fighting and also made to fit to the end of a rifle for when a soldier has to engage with the enemy in a bayonet charge, in the right hands it was lethal! Back then carrying a knife was as normal as carrying your wallet, I had a number of different knives most of which I came by in Cyprus where 'flick knives' and 'Butterfly knives' were sold in most tourist shops. The British Army only taught bayonet fighting with the blade on the end of the rifle, they never really got into the 'hand to hand' close quarter fighting, this was probably because they knew soldiers would have used those skills away from the battlefield and the last thing the British Army wanted was civilians being cut up by their troops on a night out. However, I had been given a few lessons along the way, mostly by 'Mad Willy', who was a keen knife fighter, I still have the scars as mementoes of our training sessions. The Special Forces guys we had been working with were also more than happy to show me a few skills too, I was in no way an expert, but this put me a step ahead of most people who never studied the art of knife fighting.

Sensing the danger, I took the knife out of my pack and placed it in the front pocket of my fleece jacket, I felt the weight of the metal blade against my body, this gave me the comfort of knowing it was there ready at hand if I needed it… it didn't take long!

I had decided to get out of this area and make for some waste land and find some woods or brush to sleep in, at least I would have been safe. As I walked along I saw two lads walking on the opposite side of the road, they were Turkish looking men in their 20's, they dressed in dark puffer jackets and skinny blue jeans, I saw their eyes dart between each other then they looked at me, I heard them whisper to each other and they fixed me with a stare. My stomach knotted up and the hackles of fear ran ice cold through my body, 'here we go' I thought and I touched the knife in my pocket for the comfort of knowing it was there. A few steps later I looked back and saw that both men had now crossed over the road and were following behind me, I quickened the pace, so did they… It was time to take action, there was no way I could have outrun them with my 'Bergan' on, and in my mind the best form of defence is attack! I saw a junction ahead and decided that this was where my 'Ambush' was going to take place, I turned the corner out of sight and ran a few paces to make a reactionary gap, a fighting arc, this is an area you can move around in and react to your attackers, it gives you space to think and move towards or away from your opponent, or to disengage and run. I dropped my 'Bergan' and pulled the bayonet from its sheath, I waited…

The two men turned the corner and into my 'Ambush', I stood there open armed, chest pushed out, I was trying to make myself look bigger, in my right hand I hand the bayonet protruding upwards from my fist, I wanted to dominate them, use 'Speed Aggression and Surprise' to put them on the back foot and gain the advantage of fear!

"FUCK OFF! STOP FOLLOWING ME OR I WILL FUCKING KILL YOU!"

They both stopped dead in their tracks and their eyes opened like saucers! I took a step back into a 'boxer stance' and switched the bayonet from facing upwards to facing downwards in the fist, this enabled me to punch, stab and slash any attacker that fancied his chances. The two men separated in an attempt to surround me and attack from different angles, I countered by moving towards them in my 'boxer stance', taking the fight to them and not backing down. I added more verbal aggression too,

"BACK OFF, FUCK OFF!"

My blood was up and adrenaline was pumping through my body, I was ready to fight, my feet no longer hurt and the weight of my 'Bergan' was no longer there to slow me down. My eyes darted from target to target as the two men tried to move in on me, if they moved forwards, I moved towards them with aggression, after a few attempts they backed off, they realised that I was willing, and knew how to use the bayonet. They glanced at each other, stepped back a few paces and turned on their heels running off back the way they had come. This wasn't over and I knew I had to get to safety, so, whilst I still had the energy I hauled my 'Bergan' on my back for the 100th time that day and made off into the night. I moved into the shadows of the buildings to observe what reaction my 'Ambush' on the two 'Robbers' was about to cause, I saw in the distance what appeared to be a 'Hostel', I couldn't be sure, but I did see the two 'Robbers' talking to a group of similar aged men and pointing down towards where I had been. Two cars pulled up outside the 'hostel' and around eight of the group climbed in, the cars were then driven off towards the scene of the 'Ambush', they were looking for me, there was no way I could have faced off with eight attackers, time to retreat and hide out until the dust settled. The cars did a few laps of the area and I stalked away into the shadows until I was far enough away to break cover.

I woke the next morning early, the road noise from the 'Autobahn' was increasing and had shaken me from my slumber, this was the safest place I found last night and I had seen signs for Stuttgart, I thought it an ideal location to launch my return from in the morning. I took a drink of water and ate a chocolate bar from my rations, I couldn't be bothered with making a hot drink or cooking anything. I packed my sleeping bag away and hauled my 'Bergan' onto my tired back and made towards the edge of the 'Autobahn'. After 10 minutes a young guy in a white Peugeot 206 pulled over and offered me a lift, I explained to him that I was in the Army and I needed to get back to camp before I got into trouble, German hospitality knows no bounds and he offered to drive me to the camp, he was going to Stuttgart anyway and it was only a few miles out of his way, what a 'legend' of a man to do this for a complete stranger. The time flew by and after around 2 hours we were in the familiar surroundings of the forests near to 'Panzer Kaserne', I was dropped off at the gates of the camp and after thanking him for my lift I strolled into camp slightly apprehensive as to what was going to happen to me.

An hour outside of Akrotiri airbase in Cyprus the C130 dropped to 1000ft simulating a fast approach under the radar, the portholes were covered and the internal lights were turned red. Thirty minutes out we increased our speed and the C130 dropped to 100ft above the sea, the aircraft rumbled and shook against the forces of gravity and air turbulence, the loadmaster did his final checks as the aircraft slammed into the darkened runway, we disembarked the aircraft and moved into a defensive ark simulating an infiltration into a hostile environment. The engines of the C130 grinded as it taxied down the runway and turned into the wind, the scream of the engines increased and the darkened aircraft leapt from the runway maintaining a low altitude as it disappeared into the darkness of the Mediterranean Sky.

My disappearance hadn't gone unnoticed and had caused a flutter of concern, some of the troops had searched the local forest for me, but beyond that my Platoon Commander had kept a cool head, he hadn't informed Battalion of my absence which saved me a lot of grief. I relived my story to him and he shook his head and called me a 'Mad Man', I knew this already!

Like a disappointed parent he informed me,

"You know I'm going to have to punish you, don't you? thank god you got back on time or you would have faced a lot worse!"

I nodded and accepted what was coming my way, I was charged with failing to attend a parade, The Boss, a true gentleman by the name of Mike SMITH, had done me a solid favor by doing this, I had known him since I had Joined the Army in 1989 when he was my Platoon Commander in basic training, he was a good leader and always looked after his troops. When we returned to Cyprus I was sent to the Company Commander on a discipline hearing called 'Orders', during the hearing the Company Sergeant Major ripped me a new ass hole, removed my belt and beret and marched me at speed into the Company Commander's office, *eft ite, eft ite, eft ite, eft… mark time, HALT!!!*

The Company Commander awarded me 7 days RIPPERS… Fuck's sake, I hated RIPPERS!

I wasn't the only one to have a crazy last weekend in Germany though, Baz Mitchell and Al Stone had quite the adventure too! They had befriended an old Gunnery Sergeant, or 'Gunny', who was a Vietnam veteran, he had taken them under his wing and invited them around for dinner one evening back at his home, this was in a nearby apartment block of military family accommodation. They had a pleasant night with Gunny and his wife, they ate well and the drinks and stories flowed into the early hours, feeling merry the boys began to walk through the apartment block to head back to camp after a really good night. As they walked they both became aware of a female in distress in one of the apartments, she was screaming and the man in the apartment was shouting and being violent. This pissed the boys off and they wondered what they should do about it? Both were quite handy in a fight so the thought of a confrontation didn't bother them, but that would have been too easy… Al Stone grabbed a nearby fire extinguisher and Baz began banging on the door… The shouting inside stopped and the door was flung open by a large American who began to boom out **"WHAT THE FUCK DO YOU…"**

He never got to finish his sentence… Al Stone unleashed the contents of the fire extinguisher into his face and soaked him from head to toe!

The lads ran off giggling like school kids, happy they had bought some justice to a bully…

"GET BACK HERE YOU BRITISH COWARDS!" shouted the soaking wet wife beater.

That stopped both in their tracks, they looked at each other and grinned before turning back the way they had come, back towards the bully… it didn't take much for Al and Baz to launch this 'Special Forces Bully' onto his arse before they again ran off giggling like school kids.

This incident had caused quite a bit of noise in the apartments and the lads were unsure how bad they had knocked this guy down or if the Military Police had been called. They fled back to the 'Gunny's' apartment, Gunny hurried them inside and settled them in for the night after hearing about what had happened. The next day there was still no word on if the Police were after them, Gunny decided that the best course of action was to smuggle them back into camp in the trunk of his car, so the two Brit scrappers were folded up top to tail in the trunk of Gunny's car, they were then driven past the security and Military Police on the camp gate, they had made it back to the safety of Panzer Kaserne.

***

Cyprus was an opportunity of a lifetime, we wasted it! The Army tried to keep us on track with adventure training and various duties around the Island, it wasn't enough though, the 'Party Island' had too many distractions for young men with lots of time on their hands. Our crew of reprobates continued to drink, fight, crash cars and steal anything not bolted down, inevitably we fell afoul of both the local and Military Police, it felt like I was on 'Rippers' for months, even the 'Provost Staff' had become sick of seeing me at the Guard Room. It was time for me to leave Cyprus, we still had nearly a year left of the tour and I didn't fancy spending that at the Guard Room, I needed to be a real soldier and this wasn't the place to do it. An advert had been posted on the Company notice board asking for volunteers to join The

Duke of Edinburgh Royal Regiment on a six-month tour of South Armagh in Northern Ireland, the infamous 'Bandit Country' where the IRA had a reputation for being ruthless killers… I signed up without hesitation!

PROBATIONER

(A Student Police Officer)

I had grown up as the son of a Police Officer and had suffered socially as a result, I had the constant **"you should know better you're a policeman's son"** from judgemental adults, or the **"Don't trust him he's a coppers son"** attitudes from kids and criminals. This did nothing to give me any motivation to be a Police Officer, if anything it drove me into the arms of criminality, I had more interest in joining the military and the thought of joining the Police was far from my life plan. I was destined to be a soldier and nothing, especially school was going to get in my way. In my last year at school I rarely bothered with my work and would have rather bunked off school over the woods than do my coursework. As expected, my exam results were rubbish and I left school with nothing but a head full of dreams, thankfully that was just what the Army was looking for…

After 8 years' service I was leaving the Army, I wanted to settle down and have a family, but I never imagined myself in the Police. I had been a soldier who had been a bit of a thug and a petty thief for years, I called cops 'pigs' and avoided any friendly interaction with them, they were my enemy!

The search for employment commenced and I eventually found a job as a factory worker at the local brick works, the pay was rubbish and the conditions were terrible, I spent hours covered in brick dust and was given menial tasks like sweeping the floors or digging out waste from under the machines. I had no respect for my managers, they had spent their lives in this factory whilst I had served my country and travelled the world! The hatred and an inner anger boiled up inside me, the work was mind numbing, repetitive and felt to me like I had no purpose in life. To add to this frustration I was struggling to build friendship networks, I just didn't like civilians, they didn't get my dark humour and they just didn't have the same bond that I had formed through adversity with my 'brothers' that I had left behind in the Army. I recall breaking down in tears after a few drinks one night in despair at my situation, I had gone from being a leader who was able to take men into battle to being a dick head who was only allowed to sweep up dust off the brick factory floor! Deep down I knew leaving the Army was a big mistake! I was missing the lifestyle and the structure I had been used to since I had joined at 17 years old. I missed my mates who I had grown up with, and I definitely missed having no bills or commitments! I had learnt very quickly that life in the civilian world was harsh and ruthless and the Army had actually sheltered me within their family cocoon with 3 meals a day, accommodation and monthly pay, I really didn't have a care in the world and never knew how good I had had it till it was too late. You wouldn't get a bollocking off the Sergeant Major for being late in civilian life, you would have got the sack! If your rent wasn't paid you would have been evicted! No food in the cupboards you went hungry! Soldiers are often put in harm's way so they live in this protective cocoon for a reason, they need to be focussed on the job at hand, fighting! They need to be well fed, healthy and fit, because one day they will be asked to pay the ultimate price for it with their lives. However I was no longer a Soldier and I knew I was better than this place so I continued to look for a more suitable job. Going back to the Army was an option but it was also admitting failure, I had seen soldiers re-join the Regiment after failing in 'Civvie street' and they would have got a lot of stick for not being able to 'Hack it'. Most of those that re-joined never left and spent the rest of their lives in the Army as a career soldier, a 'super lifer', who would have never ventured into the civilian world again until forced to by retirement, I didn't want to be that guy.

Bills had to be paid and I wasn't about to just curl up in a ball and feel sorry for myself! After a couple months I found a job in the local shopping centre as a security guard, the pay and conditions were better than the brick factory and I didn't have to go home with lungs and nostrils full of thick brick dust that I coughed up in the shower. The Headquarters for this company was just outside London in a big manor house and they sent you there for a week's training. The company issued us with light brown American style Police uniforms and during the week they taught us unarmed arrest techniques, criminal law, firefighting and they ran us around their assault course like soldiers, it was like being back in the army for a week, and I loved it. On completing the training I was assigned to a large C&A clothes store in my local town and was extremely impressed with the amount of positive attention I had from the ladies that worked there, the older ladies fed me home baked cakes, and the younger ones flirted with me, who am I to complain? This job also put me in direct contact with the Police and other security officers who were all very likeminded. We ran the town centre security like a military operation using allocated callsigns on our two-way radios which we used to let each other know when the shop lifters were in town, or to call for help if we were in trouble. On hearing the call for help we ran from our shops to assist each other to make an arrest of a violent suspect, it was not uncommon to end up with a drug addicts HIV blood all over your clothes and hands or a cracked rib from a violent struggle.

I was soon head hunted by the Manager of the BHS store, he had seen my potential and wanted a new Loss Prevention Manager, this was a very grand title for a Store Detective! I had my own secure CCTV room and a detention room where we kept suspects whilst we waited for the Police to arrive. My American Cop uniform had been handed back in and now I wore jeans and t shirt to work, I was given free rein to do what I wanted and go where I wanted as long as I was locking up the shop lifters, I set about my new role with vigour and business was good. As I monitored the shop floor on the CCTV It was fascinating to watch various types of human behaviour and how people interacted with friends and strangers as they went about their daily lives. We had our regular walk throughs who worked in the town centre, they would have always been smartly dressed and drinking a posh coffee from the kiosk whilst they stomped at pace to get to work on time. We had the older people who were just keeping warm and hoping for some brief human interaction with a member of the staff to brighten up their lonely days. Young families bought noise and playfulness at the end of the school holidays as mums coaxed their children to sit still as they tried on their new school shoes. Every part of society that you can imagine passed through those doors, some were nicer than others, and a day didn't go by without incident. It was the simple things you see in human behaviour that triggers the hackles on the back of your neck! The way someone walks into the store, or what they are carrying, items like large bags on the back of push chairs or a large coat that could have been used to conceal items within. Then you had the human responses which stood out to the professional observer, a suspects eyes shooting from side to side to see if they are being watched or glancing at the CCTV camera as they pretend to admire a piece of clothing, and you often saw suspects moving items to a remote part of the store and squirrelling them away in order to steal them later. On a daily basis I would have witnessed a crime being committed and I would have had to arrest the suspect as they left the store, most came peacefully but many tried to run or fight you. If it wasn't a crime in action, I would have been called to Customer Services where thieves were trying to get refunds on stolen items that had no receipts. The funniest episodes were when 'travellers' would have bought clothes for their children to wear to a wedding, the kids would have worn the clothes till they were dirty and ripped, the parents then asked for a refund saying the clothing was faulty. The 'travellers were aggressive with the shop girls and I would have been called to help because I was the manager that told them '**NO!**',

"Well I want to speak to a manager!" came the soft Irish purr of the lady,

"I am the manager" I said,

"**Well I want another one! I don't like your attitude, I'm getting a gang of the lads up here**" she threatened in a not so friendly Irish snarl,

"**Tough, I'm the only one available, the clothes have been abused and worn into the ground, you are not getting a refund!**"

I would have then patronisingly told them that they could write to head office if they wanted to make a complaint. This then descended into a barrage of threats and abuse which I soaked up so that the shop assistants, who were mostly old ladies and students, wouldn't have to. I was the focal point for their hate and the firewall that they knew they couldn't get through. The old saying 'sticks and stones may break my bones but words will never hurt me' was never so true. It used to just bounce off me and I quite enjoyed the abuse, it was like the old times with my Army mates, there wasn't an insult in the world that could have hurt my feelings after being in the Infantry. When they realised that you were resilient and not going to back down, they walked away. They looked back and flicked me the middle finger as they defiantly left the store with no refund, I wouldn't help matters with my big grin which triggered another barrage of abuse, I didn't care, it was just noise and meant nothing. It was a game of 'cat and mouse' and sometimes the mouse got the cheese, it was all part of the game.

It was in this period I grew out of my childish prejudices towards the Police, I was no longer that young soldier who was happy to get into bar fights and I most definitely wasn't a thief anymore, I had left all that behind years before and now identified myself as one of the 'good guys'. This step change in attitude exposed me to new people and new experiences, my friends and mentors were experienced Security Professionals, Police Officers and Senior Retail Managers who trusted me with the security of their multimillion-pound stores and the safety of their staff. The cops I worked with often asked me why I hadn't tried to join the Police and encouraged me to give it a go, it seemed like the next logical step, so I sent off for an application!

I joined The West Midlands Police with no formal qualifications which was not a problem in 1999, we had to take an entrance test, and if you passed the multiple choice test you progressed to the next stage. This allowed people of all ages and backgrounds to join, if I applied today I wouldn't stand a chance as a lot of Police Forces will only take new recruits who have degrees! On my first attempt the recruiters threw my application in the bin due to spelling and grammar mistakes, I literally couldn't write a sentence correctly. I'd spent 8 years in the Infantry where I never really needed writing skills and had lost any skills I did have from school. I had had a taste of the action and enjoyed the thrill of the hunt from making arrests at work and I really had set my goal in life to becoming a Police Officer. I had to take ownership of my own development if I wanted to progress in life, no one else was going to do it for me and no one was just going to appear like a genie and offer me a job. I started by acquiring some Basic English and Maths books and set about teaching myself from scratch, I even got my dad involved who set me spelling a writing tests. My mind was blown at how illiterate I was, I never knew how many ways of saying there, their or they're or where, were and we're there was, I still struggle now at times and if I see other people's errors I have to hold back the temptation to become a grammar Nazi. My perseverance paid off and my next application was accepted, I passed the written entrance test and the subsequent interviews that followed… I was off to Police Training College!

PROBATIONER

My first day began at Wednesfield Police Station which was on the East Side of Wolverhampton, it was also known as the G2 Operational Command Unit (OCU). The main police station was in Wednesfield Town Centre and it was a large 4 storey building that was brick and glass in construction and was opened in 1971. Inside were long polished corridors with offices branching off where various departments went about their business, there was also a canteen on the top floor that sold hot food throughout the week. We had a custody suite and a mortuary there too; both had a constant stream of guests from our local community. The whole station hummed with activity 24/7 and was a community of its own where everyone knew everyone and all their business. Gossip was like a currency that was traded and spread around like wildfire! If anything was happening in your life you may as well just put it on the notice board; If someone was having an affair, everyone knew about it! If someone had been in to see the superintendent for a bollocking, everyone knew about it! It was a big family who partied hard and worked harder and I loved it!

My Tutor was an old school copper called Russ Yeomans. Russ, who was a big bear of a man over 6' tall and built like the side of a barn towered over me at my meagre height of 5' 8" tall. Russ often remarked on how little I was and that I had action man sized uniform trousers, his cheeky London accent added to the effect of the banter and I took it on the chin, I had no choice in this matter, I was now his bitch for the next 10 weeks and I would have to just put up with it. It was Russ's job to mould me into an independent police officer who was able to think for themselves and act correctly when out alone in the public eye. Russ tried to push my buttons on a frequent basis to see if I took his bait and *'Bit'*, I knew his game so I didn't rise to it. Some new joiners have a complete meltdown in these situations and feel they are being bullied or abused, some go running to the Sergeant or the recruit trainers to complain. The only thing they achieved by doing this was to get a name for themselves as being of weak character, or worse a snitch! I had been ripped apart by the best bastards in the Army and Russ was nothing compared to these! I made the tea as instructed and took the crap off the team until the day the next probationer came… that was the rules and it wasn't my first rodeo! On our first patrol out we had to nip to Lloyd House, the Police HQ in Birmingham. Russ was under investigation for being on a team that had been complained about after a house search, apparently some damage had been caused by the Police and professional standards had been given the investigation. Pragmatic as ever Russ thought it was a great experience for me to sit in as his *'friend'* and learn what happens when a police officer is under investigation. It was a valuable lesson and not long after this I was sat in that same interview room as a suspect being questioned by professional standards too.

For those first 10 weeks I was like Russ's Police dog, if he told me to go 'fetch!', I did! I bolted off out of the passenger door like an obedient guard dog whilst chasing down the street after a suspect. If it wasn't that I'd be making an arrest for what I soon learnt was Russ's favourite offence, an 'Affray', I'd never even heard of this offence so early in training.

Russ started the arrest with **"You are nicked mate and this officer is going to tell you why"**

I would have to say the words **"You are under arrest for an affray, you do not have to say anything but it may harm your defence if you do not mention, when questioned, something that you later rely on in court. Anything you do say will be given in evidence."**

I then had to learn the definition of the offence on the way to the custody block and present my prisoner to 'Jacko' the Custody Sergeant. 'Jacko' also attempted to push my buttons and question me in front of the prisoner about the circumstances and if I had the right offence,

"Are you sure it's an affray, you said threatening behaviour?" … he looked down at me from the Custody desk and peered over his metal rimmed spectacles for a reaction.

I'd shoot a glance at Russ who was stood there with an emotionless look on his face waiting for me to crumble,

"No Sergeant, you misheard me, I said I witnessed him being violent and threatening, he was attacking the victim!" … my eye contact remained fixed on the Custody Sergeant hoping my confident reply would have got me through… I often growled to myself through clenched teeth **"This bastard wasn't going to get one up on me!"**.

As the weeks passed Russ took a step back and let me take control of situations, he was slowly cutting the apron strings and I was becoming an independent officer who didn't require a tutor anymore.

I was beginning to reap the benefits of my early years, without realising it I had been training for this job my whole life, a life of crime and violence. Being a retired thief I understood how criminals thought and why people didn't like the Police, also my time on the streets of Northern Ireland and the former Yugoslavia with the Army had greatly helped me to adapt to the violence and pressures of Police work too. I do not consider myself to have a violent nature and I am not a person who overreacts in the face of violence; however I am confident in those situations and will stand my ground. Russ was aware of this and more than happy that I wasn't scared to get hands on with suspects and if need be 'throw em about a bit'. This understanding allowed us to build a bond of trust and confidence in each other.

Russ was incredibly happy with my ability to get 'hands on' when one evening we were at a domestic incident; Russ was physically removing a child from a drunken father to give back to the mother who had called us as she feared for the child's safety, the father had been on the beer all afternoon and from the smell in the house he had smoked a few 'joints' too. The evidence in front of us proved he was in no fit state to look after a child; He looked unwashed, sweaty and had an aggressive scowl across his face and as soon as we arrived he became verbally aggressive,

"She's my fucking daughter and I'm keeping her, I'll fuck up anyone who tries to stop me, that slag aint having her!"

The father wouldn't engage in any rational attempts to hand the child back to her mother, Russ decided it was time to act and stepped in to take control of the child. The father became so enraged that he ran across the living room at Russ whose hands were now full as he held the child he was now passing over to mum. I stepped into his path as he charged across the living room, I bladed my right hip into his lower body and whilst grabbing his right arm I executed a text book judo style hip toss, this was an automatic reaction but the result of this move was that he was thrown across the room, his feet whizzed past Russ's face and he landed heavily onto the sofa where he lay dazed and shocked, I racked open my baton and raised it in my right hand in anticipation of a return to the fight ... I roared at him at the top of my voice **"GET BACK, STAY DOWN!"** ... the suspect sat there on the sofa meekly holding his palms up in surrender and only offered,

"OK man, no need to get violent"

Now I knew what an Affray was I was able to then tell him what he was under arrest for. Russ was beaming with delight as we left the custody suite and couldn't stop laughing as he recounted the event to the team, **"His foot came right past my nose, nearly took it off"** he roared in laughter... After this incident Russ and I were bonded and have remained friends ever since, after all, I did save his arse from a kicking, he will never admit it though…

At one point though, Russ thought I had been sent in as an undercover officer by professional standards to see if he or any of the team were up to no good, thus was the paranoia at that time due to recent corruption investigations in the force. I wasn't a stooge, I just asked questions that popped into my head that I needed answers to,

"**Russ, what should we do if we pull over a copper?**" was the type of question I asked, Russ looked back at me and simmered for a moment, then he replied,

"**If that happens you leave that one to me son.**"

In hindsight I can see why this and the other stupid questions I asked were looked at with suspicion, especially by a tutor who had been under plenty of investigations in his time.

This paranoia was further enforced one night when we came across a car that was drifting across the road towards either side,

"**He's gotta be drunk, let's give him a tug**"

The blue lights went on and the car stopped just up the road, we pulled the Police Car up behind in the correct road position and the driver, a male in his 40's was then invited into our car for a breathalyser test. Now I was still in my tutor period so at the first appropriate moment I blurted out to the driver,

"**I suspect that you are under the influence of alcohol and require you to take a roadside breath test. You do not have to say anything but it may harm your defence if you do not mention when questioned something that you later rely on in court, anything you do say will be given in evidence.**"

This was all detailed in my Pocket Notebook and then we administered the breath test 'by the book', as you would have expected from a newly trained Police Officer. The driver passed the test and we recorded all the details and told him that he was free to leave and should perhaps take more care whilst driving. At this point he leant forward and folded open a Police warrant card and identified himself as a Sergeant in the Professional Standards Department, he was part of an operation to dip sample how people were treated when they were pulled over. We had done everything by the book and had passed his test, he climbed out of the Police Car and got into his car and drove off. I don't think I had ever seen Russ so angry,

"Control from GM20"

"Go ahead Russ"

"I need all callsigns to return to base for a briefing, we have just had professional standards do a test operation on us, we are returning to base now, can you let supervision know please"

Russ's anger was seeping out of every pore of his body and I think I heard the words **"Fucking rubber healers"** about 10 times on the way back in. 'Rubber healers' is the slang term for the professional standards department as they wear soft shoes so they can sneak up on you and catch you in the act of doing something wrong.

On returning to base there was uproar, Russ went behind closed doors with the team sergeant and the troops were threatening to stay in the station all night and not attend jobs, such was the outrage at their integrity being called into question.

Bad cops are a minority in any Police Force, probably less than 1%, just like bad people in society! The Police reflect the people that they serve, so as in society there are good and bad people and a few bad apples will slip through the vetting process. They will be thieves, sex offenders, domestic abusers, racists, misogynists and even drug addicts, if you are one of these and have no criminal record, good finances and have references, you will pass the security vetting process. Some criminals who join crave power to either boost their standing within corrupt organisations by accessing intelligence or they use their position to prey on the vulnerable. Police Officers who get into trouble are generally good people who for some unknown reason made a bad decision on that day, they drove a car whilst drunk, made an inappropriate comment online and I have even seen cases in the media where people have been disciplined for taking biscuits that were left on the canteen table. I should point out that in the Police there are several unwritten traditions, these have started to fade out due to the breakdown of the family culture the Police once had where everyone paid into a team 'kitty' for things like tea bags, milk, butter, bread and as a treat we sometimes got biscuits. This started to come under attack when probationers were told by politically correct instructors at training school that they didn't have to make the tea for the team, and that they were no longer to be treated as the 'sprog' as this was 'bullying'. Traditionally if you left biscuits out on the table they became common property and anyone could have helped themselves, and if there was milk or butter in the fridge this was also for everyone to use. in the case of the stolen biscuits the person who reported this theft must have had a sense of humour failure and was never taught to share his toys as a child.

However most people who join the Police, and I include myself in this category, are absolute adrenaline junkies who want nothing more than to blast around in a fast car with blue lights flashing and sirens wailing! We love a foot chase which ends up in a scuffle and an arrest, we enjoy the rush of being the knight in not so shiny body armour coming to save the day! We have our integrity and we understand compassion and the need at times for a bit of discretion. That discretion may take the form of giving someone a second chance in life and not prosecuting them for a minor offence or letting a 'stoner' off with possession of a bag of 'weed' in exchange for some intelligence. We do want to make a difference to people's lives and do want to help our communities… it's just a shame we have that 1% that always let us down, and when things go bad the public hear about it and we are all tarred with the same brush.

THIEF TAKERS

(A person who apprehends thieves or highwaymen)

I had thrown myself into my work and had easily progressed onto independent patrol, I had a reputation as a 'Thief Taker' and had an edginess and tenacious spirit, I was aggressive and un-fazed by the rigours of being a street cop, I loved the thrill of being out on the streets and hunting down criminals, the use of force came easy to me and I wouldn't back down from a scrap. This made East Wolverhampton the ideal environment for me, the area had a lot of issues with poverty, and deeply engrained drug addiction! We policed the estates of Lowhill, Scotland's, Bushbury, Bilston, Heath Town and Wednesfield itself. The place just lent itself to crime, we had large council estates and high unemployment rates with generations of families that had never broken out of this cycle of social decay. Grandad was a Burglar, Dad was a Burglar and so the family trade was passed down as a rite of passage, the kids would have grown up with dad behind bars and mum 'smacked off her tits' on the sofa. However, on the estates there was a strong 'Dunkirk' spirit from the war on drugs, and the resilient women of Wolverhampton were the ones who held things together in a similar way to mothers and grandmothers would have done whilst the men were away during World War 2, they had no choice! You would have seen grandmothers taking on the role of primary carer for their grandchild because the child's parents were incapable of looking after themselves because of drug addiction, never mind a child. These strong women of Wolverhampton made sure kids didn't go hungry, they worked with the schools and planned a walking bus scheme to ensure these neglected children got to school where they could be fed and given some sort of positive social care. I met one little girl who was aged 10, her job in the house was to make sure that her mum got safely to bed and to ensure that the Heroin needles were cleaned up before the morning. This was so her little brother and sister didn't get stabbed by the infected needles whilst they watched cartoons and played with the few toys they owned in the morning. It saddens me that this was a frequent thing to see and we had very little power at street level to deal with the scourge of drugs that was rampant on the streets, I wanted to do more than pick up the pieces of broken families and low level crime that was being committed to fund it. This level of drug addiction made the area a target rich environment for a young keen cop who was learning his trade, look hard enough in a place like this and you will find crime! There was always a Shoplifter, Burglar or Street Robber out and about who is just doing what they are doing to fund a drug addiction.

I began to think that nobody actually wanted to win the war on drugs, I began to see that people were making a lot of money out of it, a whole economy in fact! Consider this, as a country we pump Billions of pounds into Policing alone, in 2021 the agreed budget for Policing was £15.8 Billion. That figure is Policing only, consider how many more Billions go to the NHS, Social care and the Prison Service! So, take a single heroin addict for an example, at some point they will use most, if not all of the services I have listed; I shall use a Burglar as an example, the Burglar will commit multiple crime's which will need to be investigated. A Police Officer will attend and take a report and carry out house to house enquiries, also in attendance will be a forensic scene of crimes officer who will search for clues like DNA, fingerprints and footwear impressions etc. The report will be allocated to an investigator, usually a detective, who will review the case and others of a similar type in the area. Lets be generous and say we get a match from a laboratory of the DNA at the scene of the Burglary! Result, we have a suspect! A team of officers are sent to arrest our suspect and search their home for stolen property and any other evidence of similar crimes, they find some of the stolen property from the burglary, they also find some receipts from the local 'Pawn Shop' where the suspect has been selling jewellery that was stolen from other burglaries. The suspect is taken back to the Police Station where a whole raft of services are now getting involved and the costs begin to mount, Nurses and Doctors to ensure they are fit to be detained, Investigators gathering evidence and building a case to present to the Crown Prosecution Service, Social Care are called due to the fact that the home where the suspect was arrested had children living in filth and poverty. The Police systems then reveal that the suspect is currently on licence and a recall to prison is generated... it goes on and it is endless and keeps happening as the addict spins through the revolving doors of the justice system.

There is also a commercial side to this, if I am a victim of a burglary there is a good chance that expensive items of jewellery, cash and electrics are the main targets of the Burglar! these items are sought after and usually quite easy to sell or swap for drugs. I, like most people have home insurance, as a result of this I receive new electrical items, new jewellery and a lump of cash if that is what is taken. The locksmith will change my locks, the glazier will fix my window, and I will feel a bit vulnerable and feel the need to protect my family, so I'll call an alarm engineer who will fit me a CCTV system and an alarm, not any system but a world class system that is monitored at a control room 24 hours a day.

My point here is that if we won the war of drugs and had no cause for addiction on our streets, people would lose a lot of money! We would have no need for so many Police, Nurses, Social Workers, Prisons and Prison Officers. Unemployment would rise and mortgages wouldn't get paid, the private sector would lose home insurance payments, less locksmiths, glaziers, replacement electricals, jewellery… A lot of people, myself included, are being paid a lot of money due to us not winning the war on drugs, so where is the motivation to win?

***

I mostly worked the Lowhill and Scotland's estate, it both excited me and scared the life out of me, it reminded me of some of the republican estates that I had patrolled in Northern Ireland. The Scotland's estate was a triangle of around 20 streets and I forced myself to patrol through there on every shift, just to prove to myself that it was not a no go area! some cops avoided it as they knew that it was highly likely they would have faced confrontation, to me it was like going into 'Bandit Country' and I naively thought I was the new Sheriff who had come to clean up the town!

The estate was made up of typical run down brick built British council houses with their house numbers painted on the front wall in gloss paint, the front gardens had cars on bricks that had been left to rot and old bits of furniture dumped on the lawns by the latest occupants who had no interest in improving their environment. There were allotments for the old folks to grow their vegetables on and play parks for the kids to play in, these were all interconnected by a network of alleyways and cut throughs. It was like a maze and the locals knew it like the back of their hand, they had 'safe houses' where they knew if they ran in there they would have been hidden with no questions asked. I patrolled these alleys and cut throughs and knew where key players lived so I was able to work out where to be to catch any runners before they went to ground. You'd often find burnt out cars or motorbikes which had been stolen and joy ridden to destruction or used for an armed robbery or ram raid. The local drug dealers and criminal families ruled the estate with an iron fist and the word 'grass' was viciously used for anyone who spoke to the Police and beatings were handed out for the slightest transgression against a criminal family. Many of the kids would have rather fought us and face being arrested as a preferred outcome rather than face the local enforcers who would have given them a kicking if they were seen talking to us, this zero tolerance of informants was in place to stop the flow of intelligence to the authorities.

Sunday afternoons in the hot summer sun were always the worst time to be working the late shift. The whole feel of the estate was toxic, it was decaying and the air felt polluted by the sweet smell of Heroin, Cannabis and cheap lager, the estate had the normal pollution that any city has too, but on top of that you often had the smell of burnt rubber discharged in the air from the nearby tyre factory. The locals were usually out on their front gardens, tops off and tattoos out whilst sat on the sofa getting wasted. Stoned teenagers raced around the streets in stolen or uninsured cars and before long police pursuits ensued. The Police Helicopter was often mobilised and hovered above with its distinct grind of rotor blades and engines which whined as it changed direction to keep the car in its view. The stolen car usually crashed and these floppy stoned kids wouldn't even get a scratch, it was like they were invincible and always escaped from a car crash that would have killed any normal person. The helicopter continued to circle and whine as they traced the vehicles occupants for us to arrest, we would make to the area and fight with the suspects on the front lawns of the run down council houses, we did this whilst trying to avoid the car on its bricks and the multitude of debris on the floor. The whole street would have turned out vocal and angry that we had dared to enter their territory and lay hands on their 'innocent' family member or friend. The threats began and bottles were thrown, it escalated and the mob would have attempted to free our suspect. With batons drawn and CS spray discharged, we crammed our freshly handcuffed prisoner, who was still fighting us and making like a human starfish, into the back of a police car. Your eyes stung from the secondary effects of the CS Spray and your hands and elbows were raw from the inevitable grazes off the hard street surface. Most of the suspects calmed down once off the estate, they had to put on a good show for their street cred and not to be seen as cooperating with the Police, we then took a moment, wound down the windows to clear the air, and then proceed to custody in a much more civilised manner.

You couldn't afford to get isolated in a violent scenario like this, if you did you had to use what was at your disposal to get out of it. In my experience the most useful tool was the radio! 'No Comms, No Bombs' as they say in the military, meaning that if you have no communications you can't call artillery support when you are in trouble! If the situation begins to escalate you need to be relaying your location and what is happening to the control room using an 'assistance call'. In the modern era personal radios have GPS and an emergency button allowing the control room to know your exact position, they also have an open mic facility so you can give a running commentary of the incident. This I am sure has saved many officers from serious harm and even death! But back then you had to cut across the airwaves with an excited **"ASSISTANCE"**, and give location **"RUSKIN ROAD"**, or if you had a foot chase you'd cut in breathlessly as you ran with **"ONE ON FOOT, RUSKIN ROAD TOWARDS TENNYSON ROAD"**. This triggered the control room to start sending the correct resources into that area and get you the support you needed, be that dogs, helicopter or a firearms team. Anyone nearby would have dropped whatever they were doing and come screaming towards you with blue lights and sirens wailing away. So not having a spare battery or not updating the control room of your location had a serious effect on your safety.

THIEF TAKERS

THE STORY OF THE RADIO

A good friend of mine 'Mark' was not the best at keeping his temper nor his radio. This was played out on one occasion when a disqualified driver drove off from us during a routine stop. Mark had been leaning through the car window talking to the driver when he panicked and decided to make a run for it and drive off... Mark had to jump back to avoid his back wheels and in his anger at this he threw his radio at the driver of the car as it sped off. As the radio flew through the open window I shouted to him **"WHAT THE FUCK ARE YOU DOING?"**, *we both stood there open mouthed as the car disappeared out of view with marks radio on board. Mark turned to me with his hands held out to his sides in a shrug* **"it seemed like the right thing to do"** *was all he offered. We were now both in a panic as losing a radio was a big thing and Mark would have definitely got into trouble for it. We ran back to our nearby Marked Police Car and drove off at speed in the area where we had last seen the car making off into. Mark called the control room on my radio, which I hadn't thrown at a suspect in a car, and by checking intelligence we were able to get a telephone number linked to the car registration. Mark called the number and spoke with a young lady and explained that we were searching for her boyfriend and that if he didn't return the radio he faced being arrested for theft, Mark was really starting to sweat now, and we thought we would have to make the official report. Luckily, the suspects girlfriend returned the radio to the police station ... and yeah we got him too.*

Late shifts and night shifts also involved dealing with the fallout from the local pubs, I recall one incident where I had attended a pub fight at the Three Tuns pub, at the time it was a rundown corner pub on the edge of the Bushbury estate. It was a late Sunday evening and they had been drinking all day, it was dark outside and the orange streetlights dimly lit the street and the small carpark of the pub. As we arrived we saw two guys pushing and shoving and a crowd of onlooker's craning their necks out of the pub door that opened onto the road. On arrival myself and my crew mate Pete took the two parties apart to see what had happened. The guy I was talking to wouldn't settle down, he began pushing at me and trying to get to the other suspect. **"I'll fuckin have him, get out of my way I'm gonna kill him!"** By now my patience had run out, in my young exuberance and penchant for violence at the time I thought a good knee to the solar plexus will take this guy down, not exactly a home office approved technique, but appropriate at the time. However… This guy was 6ft tall and I am 5ft 8inches, he was about 16 stone and at the time I was about 12 stone ringing wet! I gave him my warnings to **'calm down'** and **'get back'**, I took hold of him and told him "**You are under arrest for threatening behaviour**", he pushed forward into me again, as he did this I launched up at him placing my hands on his shoulders, whilst driving my right knee into his abdomen, the intention was that he would have crumbled to the floor and I would have control of him.

If you ever have to hit someone do it hard! As hard as you possibly can! If you don't you may just anger them and have to hit them again and again. For a police officer this looks bad as one hit that takes a suspect down looks better than 5-6 hits and a scrap on the floor. It makes you look like you are beating the suspect not arresting them…

Anyway my knee sank into his guts and had no effect whatsoever! All I felt was the rock hard stomach of a man with a muscular washboard 6 pack, before I knew it and due to his height I was off the floor with my hands around the back of his neck being carried around by this extraordinarily strong giant as he laughed like a hyena and shouted **"YOU AINT STRONG ENOUGH LITTLE MAN!"** This guy was a builder and strong as an ox, he had real strength, not from the gym but from years of manual labour! I had to resort to multiple blows to his chest and stomach with my knees as my legs dangled beneath me like a rag doll. Eventually he tired and dropped me down giving me enough space to draw my CS Spray which I unloaded into his face, he dropped to his knees screaming and clutching at his eyes as the mixture of C.S gas and propellent burnt at his eyes and nostrils. He was a blinded snotty mess and in no time I had him in handcuffs on the floor, at this his friends and family became brave and had started to come out the pub, they were unhappy that he had been arrested and began kicking off, Pete had his suspect in cuffs, and we heard the sirens wailing in the distance as help was on its way after our **'ASSISTANCE'** shout. The mob was getting angry, and I again drew my C.S Spray in case anyone moved forward, verbal abuse started and threats too, even a few beer glasses were thrown smashing on the pavement around us. One guy came running forward so I pointed my spray at him and pushed the button. Unfortunately the spray flew out of the canister, not in a straight angle but off at a 45 degree angle hitting Pete in the eye, this obviously upset Pete who was minding his own business holding his prisoner! Luckily, the attacker thought better of it as our support was arriving on scene, he ran off before he too was arrested!

The point to this messy incident is that we got the job done, it was messy, we needed to use our tools and we needed back up! If camera phones had been a thing back then we would have definitely made it onto the internet and would have been ripped apart by people who were sat in their mum's spare bedroom calling for us to be sacked. But people are too quick to judge the actions of the police with no understanding of violence! There is a large proportion of society who have never faced physical violence in their lives and have no idea what strength it takes to make an arrest using proportionate force against an uncooperative suspect, some of whom are on drugs and possess an almost superhuman strength. There is also the fear factor, if you are not slightly aware of the risks of laying hands on a violent person and don't consider what harm they can do to you then you are either mad or a liar! I see keyboard judges slating cops for using 6 officers to handcuff one suspect! The reality is one of those cops could have walked up to the suspect and wrapped his baton around their head, and then given them a few kicks before handcuffing and arresting their battered ass. However if a British Police officer did this they will face losing their job and face the prospect of going to jail for a long time. We are not superhuman and do not possess the skills of a Ninja either, cut us we bleed, shoot us we die. So using 6 officers is a safe way of putting the suspect on the floor causing no harm to them or the officers involved, we all want to go home at the end of a shift.

DON'T KICK SAND IN MY FACE!

By the time my 2 years 'Probationary' period had come to an end I had grown in confidence and I didn't hold some of the 'Old Boys' in such great esteem, I had realised that most were worn out from years of being on the streets, and I understood that, you cannot work at top speed for 30 years, they had earnt the right to take a step back and let the young lions run into battle whilst they plodded behind and picked up the casualties along the way. However, some used their position of seniority to dominate the younger members of the team! If you didn't bow down to their 'god like' seniority you were at threat of being ostracised and talked about behind your back, or they would have undermined any positive thing you were doing, it was quite pathetic really, like popular school girls falling out with the new kid in an American film. I care very little for anyone who thinks they are superior to me just because I had once been the sprog on their team; I was 27 years old when I joined the Police, I had a wife, a child, and a mortgage, I was not a wet behind the ears 18 year old with no life experience.

At this time I was still using a 'sledge hammer to crack a nut' style of street Policing, and my detection rate was one of the highest in the Command Unit. In a performance led culture a good clear up rate made my bosses happy so I was left alone to do what I was doing and nobody from the management bothered me. I'd even been apologised to by the Operational Command Unit (OCU) Chief Superintendent because he had to call me into his office.

Knock, Knock…

"Hello Sir, I've been told you need to speak with me?" I nervously asked as I stood to attention in his doorway.

"Ah yes PC DAWE, please come in, and do relax you're not in trouble, take a seat, would you like a coffee?" he said in a most friendly voice,

"No I'm fine boss, I'm quite busy and really need to get back out on the streets", that reply seemed to please him.

"Well what it is, is that Professional Standards have highlighted that you have had more than 3 complaints in the past 12 months for 'use of force', prisoners stating that you were too rough with them!"

Before I was able to reply he carried on,

"Now, you have to realise I 'HAVE' to have this meeting with you, I have no choice but to speak to you!" He gave me a half shrug of the shoulders to show he didn't really care about the meeting, the powers above him had made a policy that everyone who gets more than 3 complaints in a year has to be seen by their commander.

"Well boss, it's like this, I have the second highest arrest and detection rate of the unit, therefore I'm statistically going to get more complaints. Unfortunately people offer resistance and I'm not going to risk mine or anyone else's safety just to avoid some complaints"

The OCU Commander saw that I wasn't happy, and I wasn't, I was out there working my arse off and there were pen pushers at headquarters who were happy to take my detections but not the complaints that came with them.

With open palms of surrender he looked up from his desk and grinned at me,

"Look DAWSEY, I'm sorry that I've had to call you in! I'm really happy with what you are doing out there on the streets and I fully have your back, but I think you missed my point, 'I HAVE to talk to you', now piss off out of my office and go get me some more detections!"

A big grin swept across my face, I got it, he had to sign the form to say he had spoken to me, he didn't care about complaints and was just happy that he had young keen officers out there locking up criminals. He was lucky, I wasn't alone on those streets, the G2 OCU had plenty of keen souls who were just itching to get out of the station and get stuck in!

This green light to take action did however wind up those senior guys who saw it as a threat to their dominance! On one such occasion Pete and I were patrolling the 'Scotland's' when two lads shot out of a junction ahead of us on a moped. Both looked about 16 years old and neither were wearing helmets, the skinny guy who was in control of the moped was pushed right forward by the saggy belly of his fat passenger who weighed down the rear of the bike. The bike shot off ahead of us and headed for the waste ground at the edge of the estate, I knew this was where they would dump the bike and made off on foot. Pete engaged the lights and sirens, more to warn any pedestrians and other road users than our newly acquired 'Bandits', there was no way they were going to stop for us voluntarily. I saw the end of the road ahead where it met with the waste ground, Pete now had the Police Car almost in front of them and was slowly closing the gap they were going to use to escape with the moped, they would have then been onto land where we couldn't follow in the car. Opening my passenger door and tapping the chubby passenger on his butt was all that was required, I heard the shouts of disgust from the 'Bandits' and the metallic scrape of the mopeds body as it spun off from underneath them and into the grass verge! In a shot I was out of my already half open passenger door and chasing the two 'Bandits' who had hardly touched the ground, they were into flight mode and they were already running before the bike skidded to a halt! I knew Pete wouldn't be far behind me as I closed in on the first 'Bandit', it was the fat kid, he was going to be easy prey. I glanced behind me and saw Pete was about 20-30 metres behind us, so with a big hard push on his shoulders the fat kid rolled off balance and tumbled into some thorny bushes and nettles! I looked back and shouted

"HE'S ALL YOURS PETE!"

"NICE ONE, THANKS" Was all I heard from behind as I continue to chase the second skinny 'Bandit' into the waste ground.

Being skinny doesn't always mean that someone has endurance or any kind of fitness, it just means they're skinny! And sure enough as I rounded the next corner I found the 'Skinny Bandit' waiting for me leant against a tree gasping for breath,

"OK mate, Ok… I'm fucked, I'll come quietly" he coughed!

I led the 'skinny Bandit' back to the car; Pete had already placed the 'fat Bandit' into the rear of the car and we had been joined by other units. One of these units contained an 'old boy' who I didn't really get on with, I will call him 'Lee' to protect his identity. Lee had been a cop for over 20 years and he was good at it! he had risen up to be a senior officer on the shifts and he had been made the driver of the Immediate Response Vehicle, which was an area response car that was able to get involved in the high speed chases that normal cars were not allowed to join. This gave him the 'cock' of the shift status and to ride shotgun in his car you had to either be one of the top dogs in his world or a pretty female probationer! I saw Lee stood there with his arms crossed surveying the carnage of the moped and the two muddy 'Bandits' that were now in handcuffs. As I approached my 'skinny Bandit' must have seen that we had now drawn a crowd from the estate and he decided that now was the time to find some superhuman strength and kick off in front of his audience.

As 'Skinny' broke away from me I lunged forward and slid my left arm up through the gap between his body and his handcuffed right arm, I then placed my hand on his shoulder whilst pushing downwards! This move uses the body mechanics of the suspect and it should give you sufficient leverage to control the suspect… well that's the theory! 'Skinny' thrashed around until I was near enough to a Police Car to face plant him into the hood of the vehicle, this appeared to momentarily work until from behind us I heard Lee pipe up in his strong Wolverhampton accent,

"Calm down DAWSEY, that's a bit much aye it!"

On hearing this 'skinny' began to lurch up and down again and fight against my restraint, Pete ran over to help and between us we calmed him down and eventually placed him into a Police Car.

Once the 'skinny Bandit' was secure I furiously turned on my heals and stomped over to Lee;

"INSTEAD OF STANDING THERE GOBBING OFF LEE, WHY DON'T YOU GET HANDS ON AND HELP!"

He was, as usual, chewing gum, he stared at me and gave me a patronising grin whilst shrugging his shoulders,

"**You seemed to have it under control mate**" was all he said!

Lee then just walked away… I was fuming and felt my hands shaking with a mixture of adrenaline from the incident and anger at that smug bastard!

About an hour later we had booked in the prisoners and were in the process of completing the inevitable paperwork we get after every arrest. Lee sauntered into the office, sat down and put his feet up on one of the desks, he was still chewing gum and still had a smug look on his face, he kept giving me sideways glances and having little digs about our prisoners, none of it was directed at me but it was meant for me to hear…he was trying to push my buttons and it was working!

I snapped!

"LEE, HAVE YOU GOT A FUCKING PROBLEM WITH ME?" I shouted across the report room,

The look of shock on his face was a picture, his eyes bulged out of his face which had now gone bright red, it was the look of shock that a bully gets when they've bitten off more than they can chew!

"No mate, not at all" was all he was able to squeak out whilst he tried to regather his composure.

"Well I'm getting sick of your sideways comments and general attitude towards me! If you have a problem I'm happy to take you over to the gym and sort it out one on one with some boxing gloves!"

Lee had now stopped chewing his gum and sat there with his mouth wide open in shock and amazement! The whole office had come to a halt and their eyes gazed upon us waiting for Lee to make his move!

"No mate, I have no problem with you" was all he mustered, he didn't want to back down, but he didn't want to aggravate me further either, I then saw his eyes dart towards the door as he contemplated an escape from this uncomfortable situation.

"Well the offers there if you ever want to go over the gym!" was my final word before Pete broke the stalemate!

"WO, WO, WO CALM DOWN CHAPS, WERE ALL ON THE SAME SIDE HERE"

"Well he's a prick, and he's doing my head in" I retorted…

Lee saw his opportunity and stood up and walked out without looking backwards!

Pete took me out for a drive to calm me down after the incident, but he couldn't stop laughing as he recalled the look on Lees' face when he was called out. In a way Pete's laughter took the fire out of me and I began to regret allowing Lee to get under my skin. Beyond essential work conversation Lee and I were never to speak again!

Russ, my tutor saw me a few days later and we spoke about it, his view on it was,

"Well, it is what it is, you don't let people kick sand in your face do you!"

Russ was, as always, correct, what kind of Cop would I be if I allowed myself to be intimidated by one of my own!

MAN HUNT!

(An intensive search for a criminal suspect or escaped convict by law enforcement agencies)

If you don't like the thought of hunting innocent animals then hunt guilty men! There is no thrill that compares to chasing down a human being, a 'wanted man' or 'Bandit' as I like to call them. I don't mean like the big cases you see on TV where you have large murder teams with endless budgets for forensic psychologists and other expensive police voodoo, I have worked on murder cases and they are boring! You mostly work through hours of house-to-house enquiries or sit viewing days of CCTV footage in the hope of identifying a grainy image of a suspect, these enquiries involve a lot of paperwork and a lot of waiting around. The suspects in these cases are usually a normal person who has never been in trouble with the Police, that is until the day they crack and shove a knife through their partner's chest. They usually get stopped at the airport having emptied their bank account for cash, but stupidly used their credit card to pay for the flight they hoped to escape on. Now don't get me wrong there are some great teams out there that specialise in this field, especially in the Metropolitan Police and National Crime Agencies, local Police Forces across the country frequently have murderers they have to hunt down, some suspects do take years to catch and resources from across the world are used to locate and trace some really evil people.

However, my manhunts were on the streets where I hunted down desperados that were Burglars, Robbers, drug addicts and at times to be fair I hunted a few Murderers too. In my mind there are 2 categories of manhunt.

A street level manhunt can be compared to a rough shoot where pigeons are hunted! The police will see a suspicious character and try to stop them, there will be a car chase of an unknown 'Bandit' who is probably just wanted on warrant or holding some drugs. They will crash the car and a foot chase begins, you're fence hopping across back gardens and sprinting through alleyways, you send up the police helicopter, call for the Police Dog and direct resources to cut down their escape routes until you find them in a ditch screaming with the sharp end of a 200lb Alsatian dog hanging off their arm!

Or it can be the more quality game, a deer hunt where you have a high-quality beast with heightened senses and the ability to blend into their surroundings, they have spent years evading the hunter and know the land and where to hide, one whiff of you and they disappear. You have to stalk your prey, know the ground and where they are likely to go for sustenance or shelter, locate the deer, set your killing ground, get the creature in your sights, judge the wind and just at the right moment take the shot to take out that beautiful stag that has been alluding you for so long… After you have caught your stag you can often feel regret that the chase is over, something is now missing from your life and you feel a void where you once had a purpose!

I love nothing more than being out on my own or with a small team with the minimum of support and no supervision whilst hunting a human being who is on the run. Its crude, it's rude and it's a dirty business where time and pressure on the 'Bandit' and his family wears them down. Wake grandma up at 5am every day for a week saying you're looking for their grandson or visit his sister's house as she's getting the kids ready for school, and soon enough the family will turn on the fugitive and they will hand themselves in, or they will be turned in by the family who are sick of the Police attention. A lot of criminals lack the skills to look after themselves, so put surveillance on their mum's house and soon enough they will turn up for food and clean clothes, you can then enter the house without a warrant and arrest them! If they avoid their family you target their associates, pull cars over with their friends in, visit their best mates house at 5am and let him explain to his Mrs why the cops are calling at their house. You can visit their favourite pub, even their dealer, eventually you piss them all off…It's all about grinding the bandit down so that life on the run is so hard that they are always on the edge and looking over their shoulder. They can't maintain that level of pressure for long, it breaks down their resilience having to live with no safe shelter, no food and possibly suffering with a drug addiction. Eventually they make a mistake, they get caught, or it becomes too much and they walk into the nearest police station and hand themselves in.

This all taps into their hierarchy of needs which is a psychological theory that shows we as humans cannot perform without certain structures in our lives. If you remove any of these from that person they will not perform as well, or even in extreme circumstances survive as well as the person with that structure. These are demonstrated in a pyramid with 5 levels with 1 at the base and 5 as the peak.

1. Physiological needs like Shelter, warmth and food.
2. Safety needs like personal security, health, resources and employment.
3. Love and belonging, having family and relationships.
4. Esteem and respect, recognition and freedom.
5. Self-actualisation, this is where you have reached your goals in life and are happy and settled in what you do and who you are.

HARD STOP

So if you are a fugitive on the run you can forget about the last 4 of these as you are on the run and maintaining those in the absence of your physiological needs is impossible. All your time and efforts will be concentrated on point 1. You need somewhere warm to rest where the Police won't come, you have no money for food, and you know if you go to family there is a good risk that the Police will catch you there. If you decide to commit crime to feed yourself you are putting the odds of being caught even higher, and if you sleep in a derelict building you are at risk from the landowner discovering you, or you may encounter other criminals who may attack you and take what little you have. This constant drip will break down any fugitive and can also be translated into other crisis situations like someone being evicted, losing a job or a divorce where one of the parties is left with nowhere to live and no resources. Everything stops until you get at least points 1&2 under control! *(ref: Maslow's theory of hierarchical needs)*

SAVING DC ROSE

In the early 2000's Wolverhampton and some of the surrounding counties like Staffordshire were getting hammered for car key Burglaries on a nightly basis, there was a thriving demand for the cars which were getting stripped for parts or sold on and exported out of the country. Where there is demand you will always find an army of willing criminals who will seek to profit and in Wolverhampton there was no shortage of experienced and extremely resourceful Burglars.

Homes were broken into overnight whilst the residents slept in their beds and high value cars were stolen with keys, in extreme cases the owners were being physically threatened and the cars taken by force. The gangs responsible for this liked to target high value or high-speed cars, the Subaru Impretsa was favourite and could have out run anything we had! I was now part of a proactive team and our job was to take positive action against Burglars, Street Robbers and any significant threats to our policing area. Two local lads, Marco and Benny were causing us quite a lot of work back then, these are not their real names, even though they were reported in the local media I do not want to 'name and shame', they may have moved on with their lives.

Marco and Benny were out of control and were committing a lot of crime in the area to survive life on the run, they had nothing to look forward to in life except jail, so they were taking stupid risks because they had nothing to lose. We had been trailing the pair after a series of car key Burglaries and Robberies, this included a home invasion on the first Christmas day of the millennium in 2000, a gang of four armed men forced their way into a house putting a young family in fear of their lives just to get the keys to a car on the driveway, Marco and Benny were prime suspects for this horrific home invasion!

A few days after Christmas a team of cops had cornered MARCO in the loft of a house having found a stolen car parked outside. The officers had entered the house to find MARCO hiding in the loft, on being discovered MARCO pointed a handgun at one officer telling him to **"Back off now or I will kill you".**

The Officer, who was a top thief taker at the time, and not scared to get stuck in was now faced with a pistol and a real threat to his life by a suspect on the run with nothing to lose! The officers present at the time had no choice but to withdraw and run for cover! MARCO and a few others escaped and put himself squarely on my most wanted list! BENNY had also landed on my list as I knew he was an associate of MARCO and had walked out of an open prison just before Christmas.

My search commenced in earnest, however, this pair of reprobates also managed to slip through our net a few days later, I had seen them driving around Lowhill in a stolen silver Volvo Saloon, I had tried in vain to get through the traffic on the Stafford Road but lost them when they drove onto the estate. Later the same day we found the car parked up on a back street, not far from one of their associate's house's, this was an opportunity to observe the vehicle and catch them in the stolen car. Luckily this was a quiet back road, the type of place good working families lived and more importantly retired people, we couldn't easily put an observation point (OP) in a car without standing out, the street was too quiet and our plain cars were known to the local criminals, so were we, and even in plain clothes we would have stood out like a sore thumb. To hinder us further we now needed a Regulatory Investigative Powers Act (RIPA) authority from the Superintendent to observe the vehicle, this had now become 'Directed Surveillance'! There was no time for that, I needed an OP fast! This is where the retired people came in to play, looking down the rows of semi-detached houses that line the street I looked for three things.

1. A clear line of sight to the target.
2. Clean lace curtains.
3. A tidy front garden.

The lace curtains indicated to me that the occupants of the house were elderly, with this and a tidy garden, it indicated to me that they were more than likely good community spirited people and of a generation that respected the Police.

Got one!

'Knock, knock'

"Hello sir, I was wondering if we could step inside and have a chat with you, there is a crime being committed on your street, we need your help"

"Of course officer, come in, would you like a cup of tea?"

Perfect!

I explained that the car out on the street was stolen and asked if it would be ok to use his front bedroom to observe it and wait for the thieves to return, without hesitation he agreed and led us up to the front bay window which was adorned with some lovely clean lace curtains, this was probably the most exciting thing that had happened to these old folks for years.

Rosey and I sat and watched the car, the gentleman who had let us in had bought in some chairs and the lady of the house bought us up a tray of tea and biscuits too, this was getting better by the minute. I still needed to get an authority from the boss, so after a few phone calls and an emergency verbal authority a plan was hatched. The Divisional Observation Team (DOTS) were going to take over from us and bring their camera equipment to video the suspects getting back in the car. Rosey and I were to re-join the rest of the team to act as arrest teams in support of the two traffic cars that had also been called in to assist, there was a good chance that this was going to turn into a pursuit, so we needed trained drivers in powerful cars.

Our hosts were fantastic people and couldn't do enough to help us, they were of that generation, the old guy even got out the family camcorder and set it up for us whilst we were waiting for our own cameras to arrive, I had to laugh, the camcorder was the size of a news camera that a reporter would have used and it took the large VHS videos to record on, I'm sure back in the 80's it was state of the art.

Our relief came and they too looked at the 'news camera' with bemused curiosity, they had their smaller handheld cameras with them, which they swiftly set up and formed a 'Trigger OP' from where they could give us the heads up when the thieves returned and a direction of travel to the Traffic Officers who were lying in wait nearby.

It was now a waiting game, they could be hours, they may not come back, if that happened we would have to recover the car and hope there was forensic evidence in the car that identified a suspect...

'Standby, Standby'
It was the DOTs

"We have 3 unknown males on foot towards the vehicle"

"All 3 complete into the vehicle, now going mobile towards the Cannock Road"

Rosey started the engine of our crappy car in anticipation of a pickup by Traffic, moments later it came.

"Golf Tango Two Zero, eyeball on the car towards Old Fallings Lane"

"Vehicle failing to stop," I heard the wailing sirens in the background of the radio transmission.

The Traffic Officer began his commentary, this was also recorded in the control room as evidence of dangerous driving, the commentary would state the speed of the vehicle, failing to stop at traffic lights, mounting pavements and a multitude of other evidence that would build a picture of the dangerous way the vehicle was being driven. The commentary also allowed us, the arrest teams on the ground, to move ourselves like chess pieces around the board and pick up any runners from the 'Bandit Car' if it crashed or if they 'decamped' from the vehicle.

The intensity of the radio transmissions sent adrenaline through us and we became impatient to get moving and intercept the 'Bandit Car.' In every burst of information we heard the straining of the traffic cars engine as the driver pushed the vehicle to its limits to stay with the 'Bandits.'

"Vehicle has gone right, right, Elston Hall Lane, wrong way around roundabout, he's driving into oncoming traffic, were backing off… pursuit abandoned."

It was the right thing to do, it had become too dangerous to chase them any further, the risk to the public wasn't worth it. We knew they would come again, they were getting too desperate, taking risks that would ultimately be their downfall, I only hoped they wouldn't take an innocent bystander with them when it all went wrong.

***

It was a wet evening in mid-January 2001, Marco and Benny were still 'at large', I was out hunting in Lowhill with Rosey, the weather was cold, and a light drizzle was making the roads shine under the streetlights. The branches of the trees that lined the avenues cast shadows in the dim light making it hard to see who was about, this was further hindered by car lights that bounced off the wet surface as we drove. Being on the proactive team Rosey and I were back out on plain clothes patrol, we were in the jeans and t shirt gang, this is a half-way house between being uniformed cops and Detectives in suits. We drove around the estate in an old knackered Rover 75 that struggled to pull out of junctions, it was so slow that you nearly died trying to get out on a busy roundabout. Police Cars, especially the plain cars, are filthy workhorses, layers of dust lay across the dashboards and the ash trays were full and the foot wells were littered with food wrappers. The boot was full of property bags and bits of dirty paperwork that had been left in there by other cops after jobs. Basically it was a heap of crap and we had asked for it to be replaced, but a new car never came, so we had to use what we had. I was driver and Rosey was in the jump seat as front seat passenger and observer, his job was to be first out if we spotted anyone and to intercept them before they had a chance to run. Rosey was about 30 years old and a powerful lad who could have taken someone down with ease, in a previous life he had been a kickboxing instructor. Rosey had been bought up in Wolverhampton in a white working-class family and was nowhere near the silver spoons when they were handed out! He took no crap off anyone and it was always reassuring to have him with you when things got tasty.

We hadn't been out of the station for long and had made our way through the estate passing by a few of the addresses where we knew these rascals had family. Our personal radios crackled into life! a member of the public had reported a stolen car dumped on their street and two lads had run off towards Lowhill Crescent. The car that had been dumped was the same stolen car that I had seen BENNY in a few days before, we were near there!!! They were described as two skinny white lads, one taller than the other who had blonde hair, **"That'll be BENNY"** I said to Rosey! This information sparked our senses into overdrive and we began to plot where they could have been heading! **"BENNY's dad lives near there, where does MARCO's mum live?"** I only asked so that I was able to plan where to search, it was late now and we knew they would be after food and shelter... The car engine stuttered across the roundabout at the bottom of the hill that led up to Lowhill Crescent, the road was a short dual carriageway, and this opened up our view to the road ahead where we saw two figures dashing across from the right!

"THAT'S MARCO AND BENNY!" I shouted!

The two figures ran from the shadows to our right and across the front of us into the wide mouth of the road to our left. Rosey undid his seatbelt and tilted his body to the left whilst holding the car door half open in anticipation of a quick exit from the vehicle and a foot chase. I drove about 10 metres into the junction and screeched to a halt, this wasn't intentional, but because of a mix of my adrenaline that made me overcompensate with my breaking foot and the wet road surface. Rosey launched from the jump seat out onto the wet road shouting

"STOP POLICE, STAND STILL!"

We knew they never would stop, and that was why I remained in the vehicle, I was poised to speed forward and maybe cut at least one of them off. As Rosey ran forward the pair split, BENNY ran off up the hill without hesitation, he knew that if he were caught he would go back to jail. But MARCO had other ideas, he had pulled it off before so why not try again? MARCO ran a few steps and whilst looking back in Rosie's direction he spun around on his left foot and drew his right hand across his body to his waistband. His right hand came back up, but it was now holding a dark object, I saw the distinctive square shape of the top slide and clearly saw what I believed was a semi-automatic pistol, this pistol was aimed directly at Rosey!

Rosey had come to an abrupt halt! He held his hands up in submission with his palms facing towards MARCO who was screaming at the top of his voice **"FUCK OFF, GET YOUR FUCKING HANDS UP OR I WILL FUCKING KILL YOU!"** he was in a rage and using the pistol as a pointer and jabbing it towards Rosey! Rosey was starting to crouch and bend at the knees, why was MARCO ordering him to his knees? Would I now be witness to an execution? The thought of my friend being executed sent shivers through my body, panic was setting in at this escalating situation and my body began to go into fight or flight response, I had to do something, I couldn't just let the fear take over!

At this point the world went into slow motion…

MARCO was about 25-30 metres away from me… I engaged the first gear and increased the revs on this knackered out Rover 75, I couldn't risk this going wrong! I released the clutch and the car jerked forward, thank God! The tyres made a gravelly squeal on the wet tarmac surface as the car launched towards MARCO… MARCO saw what was happening and began to turn away and run up the road and onto the pavement, he now had his body half turned and the pistol in his left hand which was now pointing directly at me! As I closed in I began to lower my body in the car seat peaking just above the steering wheel. I saw the square shape of the front of the pistol and the round front of the barrel that protruded from it, I squinted my eyes and tensed my body in anticipation of the explosive flash that would have come from a shot being fired. I had made myself a smaller target, but I knew that if a 9mm round came through the windscreen it could ricochet around the interior and still kill me, or maybe I would have been covered in a hail of glass shards that would have cut me to shreds.

MARCO still had the pistol pointing at me as the front left side of the car impacted with him, the impact flipped him upwards like a ragdoll. His body flew up and backwards landing with a heavy thump of impact into the windscreen causing it to crack and implode. I felt the wheels of the car mount the kerb and this threw me back up in the seat of the car which I was now out of control of! I hit the kerb which bounced the car onto the pavement which then bounced the car through a wooden picket fence and through a small front garden, I was franticly trying to break and steer but the car was now skidding on the wet lawn… Hot steam burst from the radiator of the car as it impacted with a low brick wall, the front of the car crumpled making a metallic buckling sound as it jolted to a halt. The impact with the wall then jettisoned MARCO from the windscreen about ten metres across the garden and onto the lawn in front of me!

As the oily steam cleared I could make out through the cracked windscreen the outline of a motionless body!

He's dead Oh Fuck Oh Fuck, he's dead I thought!!!

"ASSISTANCE… LOWHILL CRESCENT, IVE JUST RUN OVER MARCO WITH MY CAR, HE HAD A GUN POINTED AT US WE NEED MORE RESOURCES AND AN AMBULANCE" the assistance shout went out across the radio!

I'd had the wind knocked out of me and had to gather my thoughts and assess if I was able to safely get out of the car. There was steam coming from the engine and through the shattered windscreen I saw the front of the car was crumpled like a discarded soft drinks can. I was able to move my legs and arms and I couldn't feel any pain or bleeding! I was stunned and a bit disorientated but I felt ok. I undid my seat belt and opened the car door planting my feet onto the front lawn that I had just ploughed through. Rosey came running bye, he wasn't saying anything but looked serious and determined to get to MARCO. MARCO was laying in the garden motionless and groaning, he had no shoes on which puzzled me at first but it soon became apparent that I had hit him so hard with the car that his shoes had flown off his feet! We assessed the injuries to MARCO and saw that there wasn't much we could do, he was however making a lot of noise,

"OK mate, calm down you're not going to die, you're making too much noise to die"

I had little sympathy, but I knew I had to look after him.

He was conscious, breathing and making a lot of noise, that's usually a good indicator that the casualty wasn't going to die. We kept him in the position he landed and waited for the Paramedics to arrive.

Nearby on the street I saw the handgun that MARCO had been pointing at us, I went over to recover it and keep it safe for evidence. I was expecting a large crowd to start congregating, I'd already had a gobby local shouting at me

"Oi that's a bit excessive aint it,"

I showed him the handgun.

"He had a gun what do you expect?"

This seemed to shock him and he got in his car and drove off, however, if a crowd had started to form we would be in trouble! This was our only proof that MARCO had a gun, so we had to secure the scene. A similar incident had happened in Birmingham weeks before and the crowd took the gun before the officers were able to recover it, the cops at that incident had a difficult time proving that the suspect had a gun and justifying their use of force.

I heard the sirens wailing in the distance, the cavalry was on its way!

"It's a fucking fake, a fuckin fake" I said to Rosey in disgust! **"The little shit has been running around threatening us with a fake gun"**. The weapon certainly looked real, it was black in colour with the correct proportions and design, everything about it looked real! Even the firearms officers that turned up to make the weapon safe said **"If he had pointed that at me I would have shot him dead!"** In a situation like this and especially when a firearm is in the hands of a violent criminal you do not have time or the option of examining what was in their hands. These replica weapons are designed to look real and if someone ever pointed one at you, you have a split second to decide, fight or flight! I chose fight!

It was only now that I started to feel the chill of the night and I noticed that I was rambling and talking crap to anyone that would listen, I was bursting at the seams with adrenaline and it would take a while for me to come down from this high! Rosey was quiet and subdued and the colour had drained out of his face. We had both just been through what was a traumatic experience, people can go through their whole lives and never experience something like this, we were both in 'shock' and were processing it in very different ways! Rosey was a family man at heart and had never had any dealings with firearms in his life, this was a significant event where maybe for the first time ever he had truly feared for his life and was now considering the consequences for his family if he had been killed! He had then seen me run down and potentially kill the armed suspect in a most violent and aggressive way. I saw he was deteriorating rapidly and asked one of the medics to check him over before he got too far down that tunnel.

I think being a Soldier had de sensitised me enough to process the incident at the time, I had served on active duty and rehearsed for years on realistic training exercises where the outcome was a dead enemy! There is no such thing as a tough guy in this type of scenario, there is trained and untrained, I had been trained to take action and kill my enemy, be that with a rifle, bayonet or my bare hands. Only then would I have dealt with the aftermath of the battle such as casualty evacuation, prisoners of war and preparing for counterattack.

MARCO was charged with the firearms offences and threats to kill, he pleaded guilty to these charges and received a hospital order due to his mental state, this meant he would have to stay in a secure unit until they felt he was safe to be released. The only injury I am aware he had from the incident was a cracked pelvis, which in the circumstances is a lucky outcome. I hold no ill feeling towards MARCO, he was a young man who had been bought up in a dysfunctional environment with poor role models, I only hope that he got the help he needed!

I also hope that he remembers this day every wintertime when his pelvis aches in the cold, it would serve as a little reminder not to play stupid games, because if you do, you win stupid prizes!

A few days after this incident we smashed through the front door of an address in the next street where BENNY had been hiding. He was in shock and awe as the proactive team dragged him out of the bunk bed and into handcuffs… he was returned to a more secure prison soon after.

UNDERCOVER

(Secretly obtaining information for the Government or the Police)

"You will be expected to covertly infiltrate criminal networks to gain intelligence, and where available purchase commodities that are criminal in nature." The advert explained,
" The applicant should be willing to work in high-risk environments and have the ability to show resilience and the ability to think on their feet."

Now this sounded like my cup of tea! But I still didn't really know what it was I would be doing, it was vague but exciting, I was near to the end of my 2-year probation when I saw the advert at work for something called a 'Test Purchase Officer'. This made my balls tingle a bit and gave me that feeling of excitement you get when you know there's an adventure on the horizon.

I went and tapped on my Sergeants door and asked what the job was all about?

"Shut the door, let's have a chat"

He then explained that I would be expected to be deployed across the country to infiltrate drug networks as an undercover officer, I would buy drugs from the dealers and then give evidence at court against the people who supplied them to me.

I was instantly sold! I wanted this job; it gave me everything I thought being a cop was all about! I had images of being the smelly 'Mick Belker' from Hill Street Blues, which was an 80's police show set in a rough American City, 'Belker' would go out arresting drug dealers and scum bags dressed up as a tramp, I was going to be my version of 'Belker'!

I began the application process which consisted of the usual stuff including why you think you are suitable for the role in 200 words, I struggled with this part as I had very little police experience at this time. You also had to submit a photo of you wearing 'street clothes.' What I didn't realise at the time was both my lack of experience and the fact I looked like a complete skinhead thug actually went to my advantage! They were looking for people who didn't 'stink like a cop', they didn't want the seasoned detectives or uniformed officers who were too institutionalised not to act like Police Officers. I was fresh out of training, had an attitude and didn't talk or look like a cop, I was also a short arse at 5'8" having just snuck in over the height restrictions we had back then.

Next phase was an interview with 3 of the Covert Policing Team, they asked about my background, what I thought the job entailed and then asked me

"If you were a drug dealer and you wanted to run a criminal network, how would you do it?"

I replied that I would run it in a similar way as the IRA do by having a command structure with captains below me who control the dealers, I was never to come in contact with the product! I would have set up several contactless pick up and drop off points for the drugs and the cash! I would also ensure that the street dealers had disposable phones and used push bikes to move around so the police would find it hard to catch them. No dealer would have known who the real boss is and no dealer knew if other street dealers were part of the same organisation. Any breach in security or discipline would have been stamped down on by enforcers who would act without hesitation or mercy... Again I had a few nods of the head whilst they took notes.

A few days later I received confirmation that I had been accepted onto the training course for Test Purchase Officers.

The next stage was a 10-day course based in the centre of Liverpool; it was a national course so candidates came from across the country to qualify. Anyone who thought this course was going to be running around like James Bond was soon disappointed! It was a residential course and we started early and finished late, we spent hours in the classroom learning about case law that would affect how we operated out on deployment. Case Law is when a matter of law is heard in court and as result the judge makes a ruling on it, it is used to set a precedent in future cases. In our case it was mostly to do with fairness of evidence and that we didn't trick anyone into committing a crime that they were not already involved in. This behaviour is also known as 'Agent Provocateur' in the UK and 'Entrapment' in other countries like the USA. This case Law had been built up over years of it being tested in court after undercover operations, the defence would say the evidence was tainted and their client was just an innocent person who felt sorry for the drug addict or was tricked into selling stolen property. We had numerous lectures from experienced undercover operatives who had infiltrated organised crime groups around the world, one very interesting operative had been the cause of most of the case law that we utilised. These points of law formed our rules of deployment and had to be read to us by a senior officer before every deployment!

We learnt tradecraft such as counter surveillance to keep us safe from being followed. We had inputs on the type of drugs we would encounter and how to assess and avoid risks when making purchases. We learnt about how to build a legend as a cover story that stood up to interrogation from a suspicious dealer. This was quite a tricky thing to do! It had to be believable and have enough depth and detail but like any lie not too much detail to trip you up with,

- What's your name, got any ID?
- Where do you live, prove it? Take me there!
- What's your mum's phone number, Can I call it?
- Why are you in this area? I don't know you!

The list of possible questions goes on and is further frustrated when you deploy with another undercover who has a different legend and you have to answer… why you are together?

The course culminated in a series of scenarios to test what you had learnt and to see if you had the ability to perform under pressure, they wanted to know if you had the 'stones for the job!'

Each scenario was played out in the real world, be that a car park, a flat or a recreation ground. We dressed for the product we were buying, if I was going to a Night Club to buy 'coke n pills' I'd dress to the clientele of that club. It might be a sharp suit or designer shirts and trainers for another venue. If I was buying Heroin I would dress as a smack head in shabby clothes and take on the look of a street urchin, I'd rub myself in a mix of mud and tuna oil so I stunk, this made anyone I came near nearly vomit, they would have just wanted to sell me the drugs as soon as possible and get rid of me. This was a good thing as if they didn't want you near them they wouldn't ask you questions and test your legend or invite you into their car or house. Safety is a massive issue so not going in a building or a car should be avoided, it does happen but you face the risk of being driven off anywhere or trapped behind a locked door and interrogated!

Each scenario started the same, you phoned a dealer, arranged to meet them, and then you had to get to the location and find them, this can be quite a task with undercovers speaking to the wrong people. This has also caused some undercovers to be assaulted by angry members of the public who are pissed off with all the druggies in the area. Or it has been known for an actual drug deal to take place with a real drug dealer and the trainee undercover returning from a role play with real drugs!

HARD STOP

We never knew what we were being tested on before we deployed, but the scenarios tested us in situations that we may face in the real world… one such incident involved sexual compromise!

So I arranged to meet my dealer…

LENNY!

Ring ring ring…

The phone was answered by someone who sounded like a scouser **"yeah,"**

"Hi Lenny, it's Matt, I'm after a bag of brown can you sort me out"

"Who are you? Who gave you my number?" he replied

"A ginger lad down at the bus station, he said you were sound and could sort me out "

He paused and his tone changed and he became really friendly

"Yeah yeah come around mate, we're having a party".

Obviously there was a ginger lad who hangs about at the bus station he knew! You make your own luck in this game!

He gave me directions and I walked over to a 3-storey block of red brick flats. I had to go to the second floor so once inside I went up the concrete steps, they stunk of bleach and piss, obviously this place was the local tramp's toilet at night and nobody cared enough to do anything about it. I was already checking out escape routes and back entrances if I needed to escape at speed! Last thing you want to do is run into a dead end when you're being chased by an angry dealer!

I tapped the door and my new best mate Lenny answered the door

"Come in soft lad, Matt Yeah?" he asked

Lenny was a typical pill head stoner looking geezer with a mop of brown hair cut into curtains, skinny and tall at about 6ft tall, his lean veiny arms poked out of a baggy green T-Shirt which flowed over the top of his jeans which sat on top of a tatty pair of white converse trainers.

"Yeah mate, I'm after some brown, sorry to call out of the blue" I replied

"Don't be silly La, we're all mates here, but there's plenty of time for all that, meet the girls…"

he replied gesturing towards a bed on the far side of the room.

He kept calling me 'La' the way Scousers do, it was a friendly gesture, a way of saying 'Lad' or 'mate' so I took it as a good thing.

I became aware of two pretty blonde girls sat on a bed, well I say pretty, more slutty to be fair… They were both in their 20's with dyed blonde hair dark at the roots, way too much makeup with dark eye shadow and lipstick. They both had those big hoop earrings that you see council estate girls wear and they completed the 'Hooker' look with tits like bullets, tight tops and short skirts…who am I to judge, I was here to buy drugs.

Buying drugs is a hazardous profession, especially when you face paranoid dealers or some dickhead on a power trip who will want to show everyone what a tough guy they are, it's far from easy! But I was there to gather evidence and intelligence too! You can't just walk into a fresh buy with recording equipment on, you may get searched or stripped by a dealer who's been busted before. And recording kit both video and sound is very limited and nowhere near as good as raw human intelligence! From the moment I made the telephone call I was gathering intelligence and evidence, I was looking at how an entry and arrest team would be able to gain entry into the flats, what locks were on the doors, which way did the doors open, were there any barricades? Once in the flat what threats are there to me and any other officers who end up as part of an arrest team, any knives, guns, dogs, children, needles, the list goes on. I would have to complete a statement after deployment describing the people in the room, each one in detail and assign them a reference Male 1, Female 1, Female 2. I would have to remember their descriptions using an A-H system,

- Age
- Build
- Colour
- Descriptive marks like hair style, scars, tattoos etc
- Eyes
- Face
- Gait (how they walk)
- Height

Then I had to remember to gather information that would support my evidence on a later identification parade, this had been set into case law as best identification evidence (R v Turnbull), this was a mnemonic known as ADVOKATE,

- Amount of time in view
- Distance between yourself and the suspect
- Visibility
- Obstructions
- Known before
- Any particular reason to remember them.
- Time elapsed (out of sight)
- Errors that you may have made previously.

So as you can imagine, my heart is racing with nerves, I'm trying to keep a cover story, I'm trying to build rapport and my mind is going at 100 miles an hour whilst gathering evidence and intelligence! This was not James Bond! No guns, just a skinny pill head and two hookers!

The role player was doing a great job of acting like he was off his face on coke and wanting to party!!

"So matt La, wanna party, I'm in the mood for a party" he offered

"I can't mate I've gotta get back to me uncle who's expecting me at work, I'm labouring for him" I said using my cover story.

"Ahhh c'mon, I've got Coke, Pills and these two birds who wanna get high and Fuck us! It will be a laugh" Lenny was really trying to test me.

"I tell you what, I will give you your smack for free if you fuck these girls in front of me" he offered.

By this time I had been coaxed onto the bed by these two girls who were seductively rubbing their cleavage against me and one was rubbing my leg. I was actually starting to get aroused!... This would have tested the resolve of a saint!

I then let out a fatal reply

"Well it's tempting...but"

Lenny cut me off, he sprung up like a coiled snake and screamed out

"YOURE FUCKING RIGHT ITS TEMPTING, FREE SEX, FREE DRUGS, C'MON LETS PARTY!...WHAT ARE YOU SOME KIND OF FAGGOT?"

I had to regain control and I began to drag myself away from the sweet-smelling ladies of the night who grabbed at my arms as I stood up.

I offered... "I really can't mate, I've got a Mrs and like I said my uncle will be waiting for me so I really have to go, I don't mean any offence, but I have to go, can I buy my gear and go please?"

I adjusted my demeanour to the situation, I looked down at the floor, looking weak and humble, I wanted him to think I was a pathetic smack head who couldn't get a hard on in a brothel...it worked, Lenny obviously realised I wasn't going to party, he had tested me enough!

You only use aggression as a last resort, but if you do have to escalate you hit hard, put them down and extract fast! That's why I had already planned my escape route on the way in...I didn't feel the need to escalate, I was panicking a bit, but I kept it below the surface, like a swan gliding across a lake with its feet going like the clappers under the water!

"**OK La what you need, a ten bag?**" he asked
"**Yes Please**" I replied, no point in being rude!

So I handed him the cash and he passed me a small paper wrap containing a brown dust like substance, I recall thinking how small it was, all wrapped up in cigarette paper and covered in Clingfilm so it can be shoved up your ass to hide it from the cops.

A £10 deal of Heroin is usually 0.1 – 0.2 gram and depending on your dealer can be cut with all sorts of nasty stuff that is cheap and available. The average street dealer isn't the sharpest tool in the box and they have been known to mix toxic substances from the garden shed into the mix, this is especially worrying if the user is injecting. A user will usually start using a £10 deal each day and as they become more addicted the more they will use. So then the habit becomes £30-£40 a day and they have to fund that addiction, so many turn to crime or prostitution. The effects on a family are devastating and having had a small taste of morphine withdrawal's I can empathise as to how hard it must be to get off of drugs, the 'rattle' is awful with days of fever like symptoms with stomach cramps, anxiety and insomnia!

I took the wrap and placed it into a zipped pocket on the inside of my jacket, this kept it safe and there was no way I could have returned to the debrief having lost my purchase!

As I went to leave I scanned the back of the door to see the type of locks it had, and also to see if there were any extras added to form a barricade, the door was a pretty standard handle lock. so not hard for a trained method of entry team to smash open when a warrant would be executed.

I returned to the training centre for a debrief and wrote up my statement of evidence. The trainers asked a few pointed questions about the scenario and took the statement I had written from me so they were able to critique it behind closed doors. The training team then just dismissed you and told you to go and come back tomorrow for another scenario. They never told us how we were doing, this kept us under pressure, and if we failed a scenario we were gone, you have failed, thanks for coming along. No pat on the back, no praise, nothing, this really did work to keep us on edge and the not knowing was the hardest bit!

Another day, another scenario...

JOCK

Ring, Ring, Ring...

"Aye whatcha want" came sharply over the phone line, the accent was thick Scottish and harsh in tone.

"Hi Jock, its Matt, can you sort me some gear?"

Same routine, Jock tested my cover story and how I had his number and we arranged to meet at a Café in a nearby recreation ground. I arrived at the park and found Jock sat at the rear of the café, I approached him and introduced myself. The café smelt of fresh coffee and toasties, it was part of a visitors' centre and it was quite full, it was the sort of place old people go or care workers take disabled kids to get them out for a cheap excursion.

Jock was in a foul mood! I don't deal well with Scottish accents anyway; I find them threatening and aggressive so he unnerved me from the beginning. Jock was aged in his early 40's with a shaven head and a piercing in his left ear. He was dressed in a short green flying jacket and had tight light blue jeans on with rips across the legs and bleach marks purposely added to complete the skinhead look. Jock had well-worn black Dr Martin boots on too which added to his aggressive demeanour... I felt unsafe as he looked up from his phone with a scowl and pointed his index finger at me, he growled **"I don't fucking know you! What the fuck do you want?"**

"I just spoke to you on the phone mate, I'm Matt" I said choking up as I dragged the words from the pit of my stomach.

Jock jabbed his finger at me again and said **"follow me ya wee** cunt" he then got to his feet and walked out of the café towards the car park.

I sensed something was going to happen to test me, my senses were screaming

'Danger! Danger!'

my eyes scanned ahead and all around looking for escape routes. It was a large park and I was quite a runner back then so I knew I could have got away if needed. We entered the car park and Jock led me to the back end away from the crowds. I saw a large green box van, the type deliveries come in with a roller shutter back, the van looked battered and well used with scrape marks down the side. The roller doors were open and in-between the metal rolled up slats of the door I saw road dirt and grease all clogged up together after years of use. There was another lad stood by it and Jock shouted to him "**You ready? Another cunt who wants gear**"

The roller doors were open and Jock told me to follow him in, looking inside I saw some large boxes and the inside was quite light as the roof was fibreglass and light passed through keeping the back of the van well lit, my danger senses were now in overdrive. Rather than committing to getting fully in the van I stayed on the metal step at the back, Jock must have thought that I was in and he turned around holding a baseball bat" **Right ya fucking cunt who the fuck are ya**" he screamed! He started waving the bat around smashing it against some large cardboard boxes, the second guy tried to push me into the back of the van and shut the roller shutters down. With adrenaline already coursing through my veins I was ready for this and I went into autopilot. I jumped back off the van step and dropped the second guy with my left leg behind his legs and an open-handed shove to his shoulders, he went down like a bag of shit! I spun around on my heals and sprinted off in the direction of the main road. Jock and his mate gave chase, I was breathing hard and my chest was burning, it turned out that Jock was a good runner too and he closed in on me with his bat in hand shouting and screaming as he neared, he clipped my heel and I fell to the floor, I skidded to a halt in the gravel and felt the pain in my hands and knees as they grated through the stones, I knew I would have cuts and grazes, but that was the least of my cares as Jock was now stood over me with the bat ready to swing at me. No time to waste, I swung my right leg around chopping into Jock's lower calf just above the left ankle, the effect was immediate! Jock let out a loud scream as his leg left the ground enough to take his balance out of sync. Jock smashed into the ground landing with a heavy 'whump' sound that a body makes when it involuntarily lands hard and knocks the wind out of you! I had seconds as the other guy had now recovered and was closing in on me, this was now real to me and beyond any training scenario, I genuinely thought these guys were going to kill me. I scrambled to my feet struggling to get a hold on the gravel carpark floor, my body tumbled forward and my legs finally caught up with me. I had the advantage I needed and I sprinted off leaving Jock and his mate behind… I finally got away, my heart was pounding through my chest and I felt burning in my throat right down to my lungs, my hands and knees were shredded from the floor.

I felt that I had failed at this point, I hadn't made a drugs purchase and I had obviously done something to upset the role players. I thought **"This is it I'll be packing my bags tonight"** and I returned to the debrief feeling battered, broken and expecting to get my marching orders, I was devastated… but wrong.

It was revealed to me that the plan was to trap the students in the van and keep them prisoner until they cracked under threat of violence by Jock and his swinging bat. I had been the only one to escape, and Jock, who was an ex-Royal Marine Commando, was ecstatic at my performance and slightly embarrassed that he had squealed like a girl when I dropped him. We worked together a few times after this on live deployments and I learnt a lot from him, it turned out Jock was a big softy really and a top class undercover officer too!

I had passed, I was ready for real deployment, I felt elated and proud of what I had achieved but it wasn't the type of news you can tell people. This was probably one of the hardest courses I had ever been on and I was only allowed to tell the wife. People at work knew where I had been but I wasn't allowed to go back on division and start bragging about it, I was an undercover! If I was needed I would get a call from a controller asking if I wanted to deploy, if I agreed the controller would square it with the divisional commander! I would have just disappeared, nobody would know where I was or what I was doing, which did really piss my boss off, but there was nothing he could do about it, which pissed him off even more!

So maybe there was a little bit of the James Bond about it after all!

FIRST BLOOD

(The first damage inflicted on an opponent in a conflict)

The job centre office in Bath was an eye sore and a blot on what is a beautiful City, it was a huge concrete building with large grey steps that led to the entrance. It had the look of post war Britain where we had tried in the 1950's & 60's to rebuild using concrete and space age looking buildings. It just made this part of the city look grey and cold and was out of place in this Roman Spa town. We knew that on benefits day or pay day as the smack heads called it, there were going to be loads of users and dealers outside the job centre! Once there it didn't take us long to spot 'Mickey' hanging around, he was being friendly and nodded at me whilst he dragged on a fag. I just blurted it out,

"Mate we aint from around here, y'know where we can score some smack?"

He didn't appear surprised or even bothered by my question,

"Yes mate, I'm going myself when I've got my giro, just hang on here whilst I cash it in".

Mickey was confident he could help us and said he was going to take us to the guy who sorts him out. Although it was only a short distance away it took us some time to get there, I had told Mickey that I had an injured leg so I couldn't go fast, he was really good about it and kept chatting all the way. We walked past the iconic sites of the city like the Roman Baths and the large houses on the Royal Crescent where people paid millions of pounds to live. Mickey joked that some of these houses had bedsits in their loft spaces, they were being used to home the towns growing population of drug users at public expense! Bath is a large Spa City with a very affluent community and it has a large tourist industry with millions of visitors every year, as with a lot of these types of places they were a magnet for street beggars who needed to fund their Heroin addiction, the locals had had enough of all the crime and all the street beggars, I'm sure they were sick of having them living on Millionaire's row too, so that's where Deano and I came in. This was my first deployment and I had been put with Deano as he was an old hand and knew the ropes well. Deano was a half Italian half Irish lad from Bradford, we had never worked together before, but we got on immediately! We had remarkably similar characters and we approached our work with a great balance of risk and humour. We were both chatty and thought we could charm the knickers off any girl around, in our down time we would drink in the hotel bar and end our nights laughing like idiots at each other's stupid shenanigans, Deano was especially impressed one night when I left the en-suite toilet door open in our room to take a dump, this was beyond his reality and he was physically sick, heaving up his guts and protesting far too much! This was just normal behaviours for an ex-soldier like me, I couldn't see his problem.

The surveillance team who were monitoring us had a clear view of us and held back so as not to show out, this is why I had pretended to have a bad leg so as to slow him down and allow the team to box around us. Safety is key in these deployments; the surveillance team are there more for our protection than evidence gathering, if things went wrong we had an intervention team that would move in and beat the crap out of anyone who got in their way!

Mickey was around 21 years old of slight build with a scruffy but clean enough look about him. His hair was blonde and cut short shaven with a couple tufts left on top for style. He wore a black combat jacket, light blue jeans, and a pair of worn in Dr Martin Boots with yellow laces in. He was on the dole and living in the town in a bedsit paid for by the government, he had been bought up as a 'pad brat' as he called it. This was the name for kids whose parents were in the Army and lived on camp. Mickey had fallen in with the drugs crowd as he grew up and his dad who was a Sergeant in the Artillery had kicked him out because of the shame it had bought on him. I guessed there was more to the story and some of Micky's shitty behaviours probably didn't help… Anyway Mickey was now a 'smack head' and currently my best mate as he was about to get me in with a new dealer.

When we had arrived at the flats I handed over a £10 note to Mickey, so did Deano, Mickey approached the intercom on the outside of the security door. It was a big grey armoured door, the type you often find on council flats to give the residents a reassurance of security, all it actually did was make the place look like a prison. Mickey tapped in a number on the intercom which spluttered into life, a croaky hippy sounding male voice burst through,

"Yeah man what?"

"I need some gear, It's Mickey, can you sort my mates too?",

the door buzzed open allowing us access to the ground floor hallway. Mickey had told us to wait downstairs whilst he went to get the gear, we didn't take it personally, we both stunk and looked like we had been sleeping on the streets for days, I could smell myself and it wasn't pleasant. Mickey bounced off up the stairs, we waited, but after a short while I had the sinking feeling that me and Deano had been ripped off. But the reality was we knew where to find him if he had, it wasn't like it was our money either, we had been issued £60 each at our pre deployment briefing, so we remained calm and waited for him to return. We knew the score, Micky had taken our £20 and negotiated 3 bags of smack keeping one for himself, that's business and that's the price of being a stranger in someone else's back yard.

Mickey bounded down the stairs like a 'smack head' on giro day, which he technically was, Mickey was happy with his newfound entrepreneurial streak and he beamed with delight as he handed us a paper wrap covered in Clingfilm each. Mine went in my inside zipped pocket; Deano hid his in his inside pocket too. These drugs were to be processed into evidence when we returned to our 'safe location'! The drugs were to be analysed overnight so that we had the results back by the time we returned the next day, we then knew the weight and the purity of the drugs. This was a key part of the process, had we been sold crap drugs we could have gone back to the dealer and complained saying we had been ripped off, this gave us credibility. It also allowed us to see who had access to good quality product and we could have prioritised them as a target, rather than targeting drug users who were just cutting up their own gear to make a quick buck!

Mickey was a kind lad and said he would sort us out any time and gave us his number. He was about to part company with us and as an afterthought he asked,

"Are you boys hungry? The Salvation Army kitchen is open, and you can get food for £1 each…I'll take you there it's just by the bus station."

What a kind gesture I thought, but me and Deano told him we had some 'graft' to do. We were planning on going 'on the rob' and needed to get off. Mickey looked disappointed, I wasn't sure if it was because we had turned down his offer or if it was because we were thieves.

"We can meet up tomorrow if you like, we can meet you there then grab more gear?"

"Sweet idea… about 11ish?" replied Mickey, it was agreed and we shuffled off out of town with our freshly purchased narcotics.

I like to consider myself as a good person who had been bought up with integrity and ethics, what comes with that though is a conscience! Mickey didn't know that both Deano and I were

Undercover Police Officers, and who's mission it had been to infiltrate the local drugs networks. I felt guilty that this nice lad was being duped into believing we were new to town and just looking for some help, he probably empathised with our situation as a drug user and willingly threw himself onto the sword to make us feel welcome. This guilt wrenched at my guts for those first few days and I was happy when we had bought enough Heroin from him to move onto another target. I had even considered calling his number and warning him about what had happened, I knew I couldn't though as this would have put other undercover operations at risk too. I can only describe the guilt as the feeling you get as a survivor after a traumatic incident or a feeling of betrayal, like lying to a business partner or cheating on a lover and waking up the next day feeling self-loathing at what you had done. Not only had I been bought up with integrity and ethics, I had also been taught loyalty, I was always told not to tell tails and that nobody likes a snitch. The deception felt unnatural to my upbringing and personal ethics, but I was kidding myself, I was a sworn Police Officer! This was my job! Mickey had chosen to sell me Class A drugs that could have potentially killed someone, how many families lives had this drug and people like Mickey destroyed? The Heroin supplied had more than likely come from Afghanistan, so the money it raised was funding terrorism! My guilt was short lived, I was a good person, I was living up to my personal values! I was not Mickey's mate; I was an undercover Police Officer!

Once I had combated my demons and put those nagging doubts to bed my confidence grew, I still had that knot in my stomach from nerves, I felt like I was permanently in a job interview. I was trying to say the right thing without letting the interviewer know that I hadn't the qualifications for the job, and that I was full of crap. This was a high-risk type of job interview though, where the outcome meant the whole operation was compromised, and I could have received a beating just because a dealer had the slightest suspicion that I was a cop. As the weeks progressed my confidence grew, but I wasn't arrogant, I knew the risks and I always acted as a submissive 'smack head' who just wanted his drugs, someone you would have forgotten as soon as you had dealt to them. Things start going wrong if you rip dealers off, generally mess them about or worst of all grass on them! So don't do those things and they are happy to chuck drugs at you all day, every day, and that is exactly what happened!

The pressures of the deceit during this and my future deployments didn't just stop once I had finished my daily drugs purchases. I had to manage up to 5 different cover stories,

- I had to have a credible and checkable story that stood up to interrogation by streetwise drug dealers!
- I had to have a story about myself for the operational team that serviced my daily needs and protection. They were not allowed to know my real name, where I was from or any other details that could have identified my real-world existence. They were briefed not to ask us questions, but as humans working close together for long hours things do get asked and revealed. You can't just sit in a box and wait to be wheeled out for your deployment and then be put back afterwards. But these are local cops with local connections, you do not know if they are corrupt or just loose lipped gossips. They may pass on details of your identity to your targets, in extreme circumstances that can lead to you being targeted by organised crime groups after their arrest.
- I had to have a cover story for any hotel that I stayed in after my daily deployments, the best hotels are chain hotels where you get your key and you are left alone. If you stayed at a B&B you had curious owners who wanted to make polite conversation and give you that family experience in the hope of a good review. You would be 'grilled' by the owner whilst eating yet another full English breakfast and face a barrage of **"What**

FIRST BLOOD

are your plans today then?, Where did you say you came from?". The worst of all are B&B's with a bar that is open to the public as well as residents, especially in small communities! Outsiders stand out and gossip begins, especially if there is a group of you. Some people are friendly and want to meet new people and after a few months on deployment you may be happy for a bit of company. After a couple beers your guard is down and someone in your group may use a Police phrase, or just let something slip that is overheard. In small communities a compromise like this would spread like wildfire, and criminal networks have contacts everywhere! If I were a criminal and thought that my community had been infiltrated, I would get photos of those who I suspected and share their images instantly with my network of friends. I would also send some paid girls into the bar with a brief to become a 'Honey Trap' and lure those undercover cops into compromising themselves by bigging it up after a few drinks or a bit of pillow talk! In extreme circumstances I would lure them into a trap where they would be interrogated and even possibly killed!

- I had to have a cover story for my family, this was at times the most difficult! My wife knew what I did on these deployments but I couldn't give her any details of where I was going and most definitely no details of the target. Your significant other would have your mobile number and an emergency contact number in case they couldn't get hold of you. All they got was **"I'm being deployed, about 3 months, should be home at weekends"** or **"I'm going to be working the next 6 weekends, up north"**, when in actual fact you were in south wales! The lack of knowing and lack of presence put significant pressures on families and was often the straw that broke the back of many marriages, my own included!

- Anyone at work who asked what I was doing was just told **"Can't tell you mate, would have to kill you"** in a joking way or **"A smack job up north"**, when in actual fact you were buying pills in a nightclub in Birmingham. You cannot trust cops! Most cops are after gossip so they have something to talk about at 3am on a Tuesday night shift, but gossip spreads and then you lose control of the information. It doesn't matter what rank they are either, even the most senior officers have been found to be corrupt. So a cosy career chat with the boss may just be a fishing trip to see where you have been and who your targets are, this is valuable information and You don't know who is corrupt or who is being pressured for information by criminal networks!

This was my first deployment and buying drugs in Bath was a challenge for me where my personal ethics and moral compass had been tested. I had overcome this and believed that the deceitful tactic justified the long-term disruption to the war on drugs. At times, our drug buying felt too easy in Bath, it felt wrong to be buying off the local drug dealers, the ones we encountered in the main were friendly and low-level users themselves. They were just trying to get by and survive another day, score some drugs and get on with their miserable existence, I was happier Once we got past them and identified who the real dealers were. We were a small but essential cog in a larger machine, the intelligence we gathered would identify a network of drug dealing and trafficking across the Southwest of England.

My eyes had only just been opened up to this world of covert Policing, and things would never be this easy again…

MORE YARDIES

"Who da fuck are you, and who gave you me fucking number?"

You won't be surprised to hear that DANTE wasn't the only 'Yardie' in Birmingham who was selling Crack and Heroin; the two opposing sides of the Johnsons and Burger Bar Crew were criss crossing each other's territory in dubious hire cars and passing out their burner phone numbers left, right and centre to every smack head they encountered.

"Who da fuck are you, and who gave you me fucking number?"

I was sitting in the back seat of a gold-coloured Vauxhall Astra, the two black guys in the front had given me no option, they wouldn't deal through the window. I had arranged to meet them on the phone about half hour before we arrived at the Chester Road train station. The city trains clattered overhead whilst we stood waiting under the railway bridge that crossed the Chester Road in the drizzly rain, it was the type of warm light rain that soaks you but isn't a heavy downpour. At least the old wrought iron bridge gave us some protection from the elements, we were joined by the pigeons who also didn't fancy getting wet, flying conditions were terrible, so they sat above 'cooing' and 'crapping' whilst hidden in the crevices formed by the iron works. The graffiti covered brick work of the bridge smelt of diesel and stale piss, this and the growing layers of pigeon shit made me consider that being in the warm rain may be a healthier place to wait. The trains were perfect for getting around on, if we felt like we were being watched we would have jumped on the next train into the city and disappeared into the crowds using choke points to carry out counter surveillance drills. The canals and side streets of Birmingham made excellent territory for identifying if you were being followed. The canals have single tracks alongside them, originally made for horses to tow barges before the days of engine power, they are also criss crossed with small bridges to accommodate roads and junctions where the horses would have been able to cross over to change the direction of the barges. Once on the canal anyone following you was committed to a route with no escape! A simple technique was to choose a canal tow path that would have led me onto a bridge, this wasn't hard to find in a city with more canals than Amsterdam, once on the bridge I observed the route that I had just walked along. Any potential stalker would panic when they saw you in an overwatch position and they showed out like a sore thumb! There were also other techniques like 'Dry Cleaning' where you walked a pre-planned route with suitable choke points where surveillance teams plotted up and observed for potential stalkers. One person following you was always easy to spot, they loiter and wait for you to make your move before they react, or they stumble and panic when you turn around and look back in their direction. A three-man surveillance team can do a better job of following you, but it is rare for criminals to have the access or training to achieve this, however, a good 'Dry Cleaning' route can also identify larger surveillance teams too. The goal is to run through a series of choke points that force the person or persons following to 'show out', when you have done this, and the surveillance team are happy that you have no hangers on they declared you as 'clean'.

The 'Junkies' and 'Smack Heads' of Birmingham were most helpful and always wanted to do us a good turn, they even seemed to show some pride in giving us their dealers name and offering to be our 'reference'. Maybe the Yardies were giving out free gear to the 'Junkie' with the most new recruits? An employee of the month scheme perhaps? Who knows, either way they were tripping over themselves to give us the phone number. This was almost a 24/7 business, you struggled to get a deal between 4am and 10am but besides that you could have got a rock of Crack or a wrap of Heroin throughout the day and night. The burner phones were handed over from Yardie to Yardie as they worked shifts to cover the constant demand for drugs on the streets of Birmingham. One dealer had offered to drive out of the city to where our cover story had us working in Staffordshire, just to get our business, such was the hunger of the Yardies to find new customers and emerging markets. Even though the Yardies had a greed for cash and wanted to have bigger markets and more customers than their rivals, it didn't stop them from being suspicious, nasty bastards, who lorded their position of power and liked to intimidate vulnerable drug users.

"Who da fuck are you, and who gave you me fucking number?"

I snapped into the reality of my situation; I was locked into the back of a car with two Yardies!

The driver of the car was a guy called Carlos and he was asking the questions, next to him in the passenger seat was a younger slimmer guy, he was holding two polythene sandwich bags full of wraps of Crack and Heroin. The car stank of cannabis, I think they had just finished a joint, the sweet pungent smell made me feel lightheaded and a bit nauseous.

"I told you on the phone earlier man, Dee gave me your number, a skinny black guy I met in Erdington"

"How come I aint never seen you before den?"

"I normally buy off DANTE, but I lost his number, I aint

from around here, I don't know that many people." I was rambling…

Carlos wasn't buying it, he was suspicious, and I saw the two Yardies nervously glance at each other, they were spooked.

'FUCK, FUCK, FUCK' I was rumbled!

"Nah man, not doing it, you go and buy from DANTE, we aint doing it"

Maybe he had been stung before? It wasn't a new tactic, maybe it had been overused around here or he had been busted in another city Like Bristol or London.

It was 'shit or bust' time, I had to push my luck, I had Jim nearby for back up and I knew we had an intervention crew nearby too,

"Come on man, you've got the fucking gear right there, I've got the money"

I leant forward through the gap between the seats and thrust forward two £20 notes towards the silent one in the passenger seat, Carlos wasn't happy! He turned his body which spilled through the gap in the front seats and looked me squarely in the eyes, Carlos pushed me back with a large open hand to my chest, I flew backwards and landed hard on the back seat, Carlos moved from his seat and locked me with a stare, the whites of his eyes were discoloured with a yellow tint and his skin was dark and sweaty, it was a hot day but this was like the feverish sweats of a recovering drug addict.

Carlos lent towards me and jabbed me with his massive index finger,

"I AINT SELLING TO YA, I DON'T KNOW YA, NOW GET DA FUCK OUTA ME CAR BEFORE YA GET HURT MAN!"

I reeled backwards from him submissively with my palms up at shoulder height, it was 'bust' time, I wasn't going to get anything here and it wasn't worth taking a beating for,

"Alright, alright, I'm going, there's no need to be like that! I'm only after some fucking gear mate!"

I shuffled to my right and thankfully the car door wasn't locked, Carlos was still shouting

"GET DA FUCK OUT, GET DA FUCK OUT!"

I was pissed off, I hated backing down, and without thinking of the consequences I let out a parting word,

"There's no need to be a fucking prick about it!"

"WHAT YA SAY YA LITTLE SHIT?"

Carlos was starting to get out of the car, I felt the cold chill down my spine that I knew was the trigger for the 'flight' side of my 'fight or flight' responses! 'FUUUUCK' I thought, I had fucked this up, my cover would be blown if I ended up in a street fight, they were Yardies, they were not going to fuck around, it was most likely that they had knives or firearms with them, only one thing to do, RUUUUUN! Jim didn't need telling twice and we bounded up the metal stairs to the train platform. As we levelled out from our steep climb up the stairs and onto the platform I saw a train waiting to leave, we both piled onto the waiting carriage praying that the doors were going to close and the train was going to leave soon, we walked fast through the adjoining carriage's to gain as much distance as we could, commuters looked at us with guarded curiosity, we looked panicked and I'm sure they thought we could bring some disturbance to their peaceful commute to the city. I hadn't looked back until the doors closed; I strained my neck to the side to see if Carlos was on the platform as the train pulled out of the station, I couldn't see him, but we had to assume he had followed us.

We settled into some seats and began to catch our breath as the train rattled towards the city, I tasted that metallic blood like burning sensation you get in your chest after an unplanned burst of adrenaline fuelled running, I had had the same sensation after the many foot chases I had been involved in on the streets of Wolverhampton as a uniformed cop. The burning sensation was by now a well-known 'friend' to me, If I felt that pain, I knew I had given it my all, this time however I was the one being pursued, I wasn't sure I liked that feeling.

The train pulled into New Street train station in the city centre and we began 'Counter Surveillance' drills, we couldn't know for sure if we had been followed onto the train. I knew the station well after years of passing through there in transit as a young soldier going on leave and moving around the country from base to base. I knew there was a back way out of the station down some concrete stairs, it led to a pub called the Station Bar, it was on the junction of Station Street and Dudley Street which led to the old markets area of the city. Soldiers frequented the bar whilst waiting for their connections, it was a shit hole, but the beer was cheap, and the troops knew where everyone would congregate whilst in transit. The bar was always open due to it being near the markets, wholesale market traders worked funny hours to prepare for a day's trading, sometimes starting at midnight, due to this some pubs were given special licences to open outside of normal pub licencing hours, this way they could have a drink after work, even if it was 10am… The stairs stunk of piss and were littered with used hypodermic needles, street drinkers and tramps used it as a public toilet and smack heads used it as a convenient place to 'jack up'. People never used these stairs unless they had to, it was a mugger's paradise and people tended to avoid it. The unwelcoming stairs gave us the perfect 'choke point' to see if we were being followed, we headed down the stairs and waited at one of the nearby bus stops to observe. A few of the braver commuters followed us down and a couple of street drinkers staggered along the route too, but no one of concern stood out, the coast was clear, time to call the boss and get extracted!

On our return the surveillance team confirmed what I had thought, Carlos had given up when he saw two skinny 'Junkies' bolting up two flights of stairs, he was no athlete and wasn't playing those games.

I was angry with myself and disappointed that I hadn't made a purchase, the drugs were in touching distance and I had failed to close the deal. The boss on the operational team wasn't too bothered, he was more relieved that we were safe and glad that we had got away without incident. It was good to know that he appreciated the pressure we were under, even if at times we forgot the risks ourselves. This scenario could have ended very differently if we had hung around for a fight, Carlos and his mate could have been armed, if they had pulled out firearms and started shooting or slicing at us with machete's we could have been seriously hurt or killed, and that would have caused a lot of paperwork.

The days deployment wasn't a total loss, we hadn't made a purchase, but we had surveillance footage of two suspects, a telephone number, a registration number of a vehicle and my intelligence about the bags full of Crack and Heroin. All this information was fed into the intelligence system and the vehicle was now going to be targeted during 'Stop and Search' operations, even if they found no drugs, they would be able to identify the occupants of the vehicle and build an intelligence picture around the Yardie gangs and its members operating in Birmingham.

The operation came to an end and as with all my previous deployments I had to return to normality, but what is normality? I had a family at home who I loved dearly, but the cracks in my marriage were starting to show, each time I had been away coming back to this reality became harder and harder. I was living away from home for months at a time undercover and taking on the stress of a completely different identity whilst buying drugs from some of the most dangerous people in the country. It was hard to switch it off; one day you are having a Police Officer shove a pistol in your face, the next you are confronting a drugged up Yardie, how can you be expected to just go home and play happy families after that. Like most people myself and the wife hid our difficulties, I worked long hours in my day job, which was also fast paced and exciting, so that helped to keep my thirst for action satisfied. The Wife and I tried to make things work, but we were growing further apart and my head was always on 'The Job', I loved what I did and if I had the choice of staying at work chasing

HARD STOP

bad guys or going home for some 'normality', I chose 'The Job', normality just couldn't match the rush I got from it. On my few days off we drank a lot of alcohol to blot out the futility of our situation and to try and have some fun, this was destructive and never a good strategy…

how did I ever find myself living this kind of life?

DNA

(The unique genetic code used to identify criminal suspects)

The handcuffs weren't so tight this time, but the rigid cross bar still made them dig into my wrists causing some discomfort, however, my knees stung and ached like a bitch. I had landed hard on the sharp gravel of the carpark, the ground was pockmarked like a lunar landscape with potholes which were filling up with rainwater, the only benefit of this was that the wet mud and gravel soaked through my cargo trousers and cooled the grazes from my landing. The rain filled potholes created mirrors in the night that reflected the wash of blue strobe lights from the Police cars that now surrounded us. My sweat soaked body was starting to feel the icy cold bite of the February night air through my light T-Shirt, it was however a cooling relief from the now emerging bruises I had sustained at the hands of Lancashire's finest Police Officers. Myself and Bish were knelt next to each other on the floor and were guarded over by two Police Officers in dark blue 'Riot' uniforms, it looked like we were awaiting execution. Others in a similar state to us were being led out of the building handcuffed with hands to the rear, they were bent forward slightly to keep them off balance, this enabled full control of them as they were led by 'Riot Cops' towards a large truck that had been converted into a mobile prisoner transportation lorry, they were obviously expecting a lot of arrests tonight. My ears were still ringing, and the carpark, although busy, seemed to be calm and controlled compared to the heat and mayhem of the tightly packed dance floor. The array of lasers and the thumping loud 'Dance Music' that had been blasting out in the 'Rave' were now echo's that continued to pulse in my brain.

Here I was again, in handcuffs, with a pocket full of drugs and free from prosecution… best job I ever had!

***

Drugs are popular for the sole reason that they make you feel good, or just normal in some cases, if they didn't, then people wouldn't take them! Your drug of choice might be Heroin so that you can feel warm and cozy in a world that you hate, a break from reality perhaps. You may drink alcohol, yes alcohol is a drug, one of the worst in fact! But most people use it to release their inhibitions and enjoy a good night out, this is healthy and most people can control their intake, however, some don't and alcoholism sets in and the once loved tipple becomes a toxic life destroying drug, look in any hospital or prison, you will find evidence of the physical, mental and emotional harm that alcohol can have. Many people on the 'Club Scene' will take a cocktail of drugs like Acid, Ecstasy, Ketamine, Amphetamine and Cocaine to experience an out of body high that brings them true euphoria and the richest feelings of love and compassion imaginable. Another thing or two that drugs have in common are, like most things, is that they are damaging to the mind and body if taken in excess, recreational drugs are unregulated in most countries and are 'cut' with any number of impurities, due to this they do not meet the high pharmaceutical standards required for human consumption. One of the worst facts about drugs is that due to this lack of regulation and control the trade is sat firmly in the hands of Violent Organised Crime Groups!

But, that all aside, drugs are fun!

The 'Rave Scene' of the 90's was still hanging on by its fingertips in 2004 and youngsters still wanted to go out and 'get off their faces' on Ecstasy as it is known, the real name for it was Methylene Dioxy Meth Amphetamine (MDMA), it had other street names too like 'E', or 'Molly'. The Ecstasy pills were usually chalky and sometimes came with a stamp on it from the producers, sometimes a 'Dove' and other times a smiley face, or a car sign like 'Mitsubishi', this was just another piece of drug's advertising that told the 'Pill Heads' that they were cool and these were "Mitsubishi Turbo's" or " Doves", I doubt they were any different to the other tablets sold across the world at that time but people bought them in their billions. The creator of the Mitsubishi logo on the Ecstasy pills was a man by the name of 'Gunther ASHCROFT', he was a Dutch Chemist and had a rapidly expanding drugs distribution network evolving across the UK and Europe. To keep up with demand he had to expand his Dutch based enterprise and he bought a number of buildings, one of which was an old Mitsubishi dealership that had been closed down. He had a few other businesses too which he used to hide his cash, including of all things a 'Crown' making factory, he was becoming rich beyond all belief and had become concerned about security, so he began changing the logos on his pills to keep the authorities guessing who the producer was. However, when he used the Mitsubishi emblem to promote his illegal trade, he had made a serious mistake! Mitsubishi took the use of their emblem as an insult to their ancient and honorable name and declared war on those who had disrespected them, their first act of war was to employ the Japanese Secret Service who, in conjunction with British law enforcement, deployed agents to identify the source of the drugs. After 3 years they narrowed their search to Ashcroft's Mitsubishi garage in Holland, a 4-hour gun battle ensued between the Dutch Special Forces and those who were inside producing the pills. It is reported that 123 pill engravers and 34 pill makers were killed in the shootout, and another 57 died from their bodies overheating after taking large quantities of MDMA. Ashcroft himself 'dropped' 12 pills, and in a drug induced frenzy he charged at the soldiers who cut him down with machine gun fire! Ashcroft has set a standard for those who dare to insult the good name of a Japanese company like Mitsubishi, the agents employed by the company decapitated Ashcroft and were allowed to return to Japan with the severed head, the head now sits in a glass case in Tokyo as a 'war trophy' and a warning to others!

But, that all aside, drugs are fun!

The Northwest's top "All-nighter dance club" sounded like an exotic place to go, it wasn't far from the bright lights of Blackpool and close to big cities like Manchester and Liverpool, so it must be a good night out if those cities couldn't beat it? 'Monroe's' was situated in a small town called Great Harwood, this was another town in the Northwest that had fallen into decay as industries across the country closed down, leaving a rise in unemployment and many once vibrant communities on their knees. A left over of this industrial heritage was row after row of terrace workers cottages where low-income families lived, small pubs and takeaways were the only source of entertainment for the now mostly unemployed residents. That was except for 'Monroe's', an old Sports and working man's club on the edge of town, it turned out to be as far removed from the 'Gods Kitchen' rave events held at large licensed venues like the National Exhibition Centre that I had been to before. Compared to these locations this was an 'Underground' club, this was where real ravers went, those who are dedicated to 'the scene' and would have never been seen dead at a commercial rave like 'God's kitchen'! The door staff were thugs who took the door entry fee and were there as muscle to make sure that only authorized drug dealers were allowed entry, and they also attempted to make sure that not too many weapons made their way into the venue. There was always the threat of rival gangs attending the events to cause trouble or to steal the drugs and cash that were pouring into the club, so any door staff that worked this venue had to have the capability of extreme violence.

Although the club bought some life to the town, it was the wrong type of life and it caused great concern to local residents due to the anti-social behavior aspect, but also due to the influx of young people taking recreational drugs to the area. It was 2004 and the country still had strong memories of the death in 1995 of a young girl from Essex by the name of 'Leah BETTS', Leah went out with friends to celebrate her 18th Birthday and during the night she took an ecstasy tablet, this was not uncommon as the 'Rave' culture was in full swing at this time and the pills were commonplace in most clubs. There had been lots of advice put out for 'clubbers' to ensure that they hydrated to counter the body heating effects of MDMA and dehydration from dancing, Leah followed this advice but drank excessive levels of water that her body was unable to process, Leah fell into a coma and died in hospital with her parents at her bedside. The Postmortem revealed that she consumed in excess of 7 Litres of water and due to the effects of the ecstasy tablet on her bodily functions she was unable to relieve herself. This led to water intoxication and hyponatremia, her brain swelled and this led to the coma from which she did not awake. Leah's parents released photographs of their daughter hooked up to life support machines and attended press conferences to tell of their utter disbelief in the tragic waste of life that they had witnessed, Leah's death sent shock waves across the country, she was from a normal middle-class family, not the usual 'Junkie' that had died on the street of an overdose, this made parents across the country sit up and take notice! Due to the outburst of national shock it was still in recent memory of people who were alive at the time of her tragic passing. There were no significant prosecutions in this case, some of her friends received minor reprimands for what is now known to be a lesser crime of 'social supply' between friends.

But, that all aside, drugs are ... you get where I'm going with this!

Lancashire Police had listened to the concerns of their community and decided that 'Monroe's' was a significant enough threat to the safety of young party goers, such was their concern they decided to take the extreme measure of deploying undercover officers! 'Operation Escort' was created with the aim of gathering sufficient evidence to carry out a closure of the venue and to identify those who were concerned in the supply of potentially lethal drugs. Myself and a guy called Bish had been called up to infiltrate the venue, it was a 'weekender' job due to it being a club, and as we were only be needed at the weekend, we would have to go back to our day jobs in between, we were happy with that, it was the best of both worlds for us. We were both Detectives and we had caseloads back at our own forces that often got neglected when we were away for long periods of time.

Bish had a kindly manner about him and I knew by his accent that he was from the South, probably Wiltshire or Berkshire way, a real 'Farmers Boy', he was well built and sported some good tattoos, I never asked where he was from, it was none of my concern. He had mousy brown hair in a curtain style cut which hung over his eyes giving him a 'Droopy dog' look. However, it soon became apparent that Bish was a switched-on cookie and his soft Country accent and friendly conversation had a great way of putting people at ease when he spoke to them, he also 'Busted out' some great moves on the dance floor!

The Operational Team were locals and had that 'clippy' northern accent that was friendly and relaxed. These teams were the same wherever you went, just the accents changed, Northerners, Southerners, Brummies' or the Welsh, it didn't matter where they were from, they were all dedicated professionals who believed in what they were doing.

The DS who took the briefing threw me a set of car keys,

"Go and find Monroe's, see what turns up, just a look and see tonight"

The keys were to a beat-up Peugeot 205 1.9 GTI car, it was white once, but now its rusting exterior gave it a hit of reddish dirtiness, the interior was grey and smelt of mildew. This was the perfect job car for where we were going, it suited us and it suited our cover story. We had decided on our drive to Lancashire that we would have to keep our cover story simple, we were new to the 'Rave Scene' and had met at an unlicensed event in Birmingham where we became friends, I only knew him as Bish and he only knew me as Jack. We lived nowhere near each other and had never met each other's families or friends, all I had was Bish's phone number and had contacted him when I heard on a Pirate Radio Station that 'Monroe's' was a great place to go, so I called Bish and we set out in search of the club. This simple story, which in the club scene was more than plausible, allowed us to have our own back stories that couldn't be cross referenced if we were interrogated by a drug dealer or one of the heavies on the club entrance.

We parked up just short of the club, I didn't commit to the car park but left the car on the street facing towards the main route out! If we needed a quick exit then I didn't want to be blocked in or have to mess about reversing or doing 3 point turns, the car looked like crap but the engine was sound and started immediately when we needed it to, this was most important as it was potentially going to be our getaway car if the shit hit the fan.

I heard and felt the deep repetitive hum of the beating music coming from the club and in unison our heads started nodding in time with the beat. The building was no more than a concrete and timber clubhouse that adjoined the towns football club, I doubted they used it anymore for football events and I doubted that the football team even existed beyond a local league anymore either. There were 4 Doormen guarding the entrance, they looked awkward in their uniform of Bow Tie, white shirt and black bomber jackets, but they held themselves with the physical presence of men trained for violence, real scrappers, probably fighters from the Mixed Martial Arts Gyms of Liverpool and Manchester, lean and ready to go at the drop of a hat! We were given a cursory search and they relieved us of £5 each for the entry fee, they waved us in and we headed to the bar which only sold bottled water,

"I'll take two double bottled waters with a slice please darling"

The barmaid, just looked straight through me like the twat I was and handed over 2 bottles of water.

Like wallflowers we lingered around the edge of the dancefloor sipping from our bottles of water whilst waiting for the place to fill up.

The strobing lights pulsed in time with the constant beat of the music that intensified and sent pulses of throbbing light and music deep into our souls!

'Bum Chacka, Bum Chacka, Bum Chacka, Bum Chacka, Bum Chacka, Toot Toot!'

Bikini clad women in glittery cowboy hats and knee high 'hairy boots' stomped on podiums; they blew loud whistles in time with the beat of the music as the club began to fill with young people in various forms of undress. Some of the women wore bikinis and others wore body hugging dresses that scarcely covered their young fit bodies. The lads hung thick metal kerb chains around their necks and wore t shirts that wouldn't stay on for long as their body heat rose up with a mixture of MDMA and intense heat from the dance floor. I was dressed the same in my thin baggy t shirt that hung off me, and around my neck I wore a silver kerb chain that I had acquired from the Police Property Store to enhance my look, not too thick, but thick enough to fashionably stand out. I added to my look with a close-cut shaven head and I had shaved 3 stripes into my left eyebrow making an adidas sign, I looked like a thug but it was a look that I needed to fit in with this environment. I didn't want to go in there looking like a soft college kid on a school trip who was just asking to get robbed, I also didn't want to stand out as someone who thought they were a hard man either, both could have bought me the wrong kind of attention and lots of trouble. I had to pull off the look of a friendly guy who wasn't a threat to anyone, but also someone you really didn't want to mess with either. This was a perfect 'grey man' situation where you were just another 'pill head', no one of note, your face was forgotten as soon as you were dealt to by a Drug Dealer or allowed entry by a Doorman!

We joined the masses of 'clubbers' on the dance floor where, with our hands in the air, like we just didn't care, we began 'throwing shapes' and 'gurning' our faces by swinging our jaws like we were finalists in the village 'gurning' competition. Throwing hand shapes and pulling strange faces was just something that was part of the culture, the 'swinging jaw' faces was also an effect of the MDMA or Cocaine that many took. Friendly lads hugged us and girls danced close as they waved their arms in unison with the beats, this was fun, I saw why people travelled so far to come here and to other events too, everyone was loved up and unlike normal night clubs there appeared to be none of the normal territorial aggression that you get, everyone here just wanted to dance and be happy.

From the corner of my eye I saw a group of about 6 lads following a guy towards the toilets and decided to follow, if there's a queue in a place like this, it's going to be a queue for pills! I only hoped I had got this right and wasn't joining a queue for a 'gay gang bang', I wasn't in the mood!

Bish followed and joined me in the line where we waited to be 'served up', the 'Dealer' was holding a sandwich bag in his left hand that contained a few hundred pills, maybe nearer a thousand?

"How many you want mate?"
"EH, just 3 please mate"
"That's £30 then!"

The 'Dealer' was a blonde lad, in his early twenties, not too tall and quite thin, he appeared unthreatened by the growing queue of 'clubbers' who bopped up and down as they waited in turn to be served pills, he obviously felt safe and protected in the club. I had no doubt that he was one of the authorised 'Dealers' that would have easily got past the Doormen!

I slid him the notes and Bish repeated the same process of 'supply and demand' as I stood and waited. We stuffed our drugs into our 'safe' pockets and returned to the anonymity of the dancefloor where we chatted under the cover of the music. The blonde-haired dealer appeared to be the only source of pills that night and clubbers, both male and female, were back and forth from him for the rest of the evening, 'Blondie' had thrown himself on the sword, he was now a legitimate target!

***

A week later we repeated the now familiar routine of pre deployment briefings, these were to ensure we knew what rules we had to abide by and how far we could have gone before our evidence would have been tainted as 'Entrapment'! It was repetitive and boring going through the rules but we had to do it, we had to be clear in our minds what we could and could not do. I have seen accounts from some undercover officers who spin yarns in their memoires about taking drugs with the people they buy from, perhaps this is 'Artistic License', but whatever it is, this would not be normal procedure for a Test Purchase Operative, you can't do it and you have to make every excuse not to do it. You establish and maintain relationships with targets to gain access to the product or intelligence, that is it, nothing more, you don't go thieving with them or go to their mums for dinner and you definitely don't start any kind of sexual relationship with them! You are an anonymous figure who drifts in, gathers evidence and drifts out, a ghost, but a ghost that comes back to haunt them when they barely remember you.

The cash was counted out and some mug shots were shown to us of local gangsters that the operational team thought may be involved, none really stood out as anyone who we had seen or spoken to so far. As we hadn't been searched properly on our last deployment, we felt safe enough to go in wired this time, so I was fitted with a small video recording device, we needed some facial identification of 'Blondie' during a deal and this was the only way to get it.

We climbed into our trusted 'GTI' and fired up the engine, we had a pocket full of Taxpayers cash and we were off to Monroe's!

The 2 doormen scarcely looked at us as we passed them our admission fee, there was not even a cursory search before we passed into the throbbing beat of the club. Was this luck or just sloppy door staff? Had we been searched and the recording device discovered, we would have been deep in the crap! The car was nearby and like last time I had parked it ready to go in case we had to get out quick.

The dancing girls in 'Bikinis and cowboy hats' started blowing their whistles, and the party had begun, soon the place was pounding out the repetitive beats of the week before. Right on cue, 'Blondie' turned up like the 'pied piper' and soon he had a trail of loved up kids following him to the toilets for their pills. We joined the queue and I activated the recording equipment… The lights in the club were not the best and we hoped that the camera would have recorded both audio and video of the deals, however, you can never rely on it so a contingency is always needed in case it fails. We hung around outside the toilet area where 'Blondie' was still plying his trade, we waited for him to finish, as he came out, he 'sparked up' a cigarette!

This simple act 'sparked up' my inner Detective! which then in turn set in motion a plan of action to obtain some unquestionable evidence of identification! To be a good undercover officer you need to be a good investigator who has knowledge of investigative tools and have knowledge of how to prove a criminal case, there is no point in going undercover if you don't gather good evidence that will stand up in court! To prove someone's identification you can use things like; a witness who knows the person, fingerprints at a crime scene, or you can use the most reliable form of evidence currently known to investigators... DNA!

Blondie flicked his spent cigarette to the floor and strolled off leaving it smoldering where it landed. I had worked my way closer to him as it was near to the dancefloor and I pretended to be tranced on the lights and bop away with no cause for him to be suspicious. A quick scan around me reassured me that I wasn't being watched, I quickly dropped down pretending to tie my shoelace and snatched up the still warm cigarette butt. I then hastily placed the dead cigarette in a pocket away from the pills I had purchased from Blondie earlier, this prevented any DNA cross contamination, I now had a key piece of evidence that was going to identify our suspect.

DNA, also known as genetic finger printing, was first developed at the University of Leicester in the 1980's, they had unlocked the genetic code that enabled them to profile an individual's unique identity. This was quickly put to use by Leicestershire Police who were investigating the murder and rape of two young girls. The investigators conducted the world's first mass DNA testing, they took samples off 5000 men from villages in the area of the murders. The investigation eventually led to the now infamous serial killer 'Colin Pitchfork', the investigation team initially failed to make a match but Pitchfork had been heard boasting that he had persuaded a friend to give a DNA sample on his behalf, Pitchfork was arrested and a match was made. Colin Pitchfork was the first person in the world to be convicted based on DNA evidence, as a result of this conviction he was sentenced to Life Imprisonment! In the wake of this investigation, it was decided that a DNA database was to be created and samples taken from persons known to be involved in crime, this was to be cross referenced with any DNA evidence left at the scene of a crime such as Skin Cells, Semen, Saliva and Blood. Therefore, anything that can capture any of these things, like a 'cigarette butt', are important sources of DNA evidence!

I was confident that the cigarette butt in my pocket was going to give me sufficient evidence to identify 'Blondie', we hung about for a while longer, we had both purchased some pills off 'Blondie' so there wasn't much for us to do except soak up the atmosphere and enjoy the music. We had now purchased drugs from our target twice, we had potential DNA evidence and hopefully we had some good video footage of our target too, this had been a productive deployment and it was time to get out of there. In a place like this anything can go wrong fast, so why hang around longer than we needed to and risk being compromised.

The Operational team were excited about what 'goodies' we had bought back for them, the pills were bagged up in evidence bags and sealed, so was the cigarette butt, the DI looked dumbfounded when I explained my rational for seizing a cigarette butt, he gave me a bemused look and with a shrug he agreed,

"Why not, let's see what we get."

Bish plugged in the recording device to a laptop computer and downloaded the video of our time in the club. With the loud beating music and flashing lights, the audio was of very little use and due to the lighting in the toilets there was only a few grainy shots of 'Blondie', in my view it was useless as evidence. As the video played one of the operational team became convinced it was a local lad and named him,

"I swear its Paul Smith! I'd put a month's wages on it!"

he then went on to pull out one of the mug shots we had been shown earlier from a box file, he held it up and pointed at a picture of a young blonde guy,

"it's him!"

Bish sighed, he was tired, and in his best 'Farmers Boy' voice he warned,

"Well before you lose your money mate, we looked at those pictures earlier, and I've been up close with this guy! It is not the same bloke!"

A clippy northern reply came back,

"I'm sure its him, I used to deal with him and his brother all the time when I worked this area" he insisted.

I had had enough of this guy now,

"OK, let's send the DNA off and see what comes back on that before we start doing any 'formal' identifications", the DI nodded in agreement with me, maybe this was because he trusted my investigative judgment, or maybe he knew that his member of staff was a bit quick of the mark and not that reliable.

***

I had just climbed the stairs that led to the briefing room, we had just arrived after a week away and were hurriedly preparing ourselves for the night ahead, tonight was 'enforcement' night!

"WELL, THAT COULD HAVE BEEN EMBARRASING!" The DI's voice boomed across the briefing room as Bish and I walked in,

"what's up boss?" the humorous tone in his voice wasn't lost on us, he obviously had a funny story to tell us and had been itching for us to arrive.

"You should have taken that bet; 'Blondie' isn't Paul SMITH!" ... "Your cigarette butt came back from the laboratory with a DNA match, he called Billy Edwards, he's a well-known scum bag from Manchester."

The grin on my face ran from ear to ear and it stretched even further when the Officer who had made the identification came in the room, he obviously had already been told, because when I looked at him, all I got in return was a clippy, **"OK, fuck off smart arse."**

I just chuckled to myself and continued to prepare my gear.

'Enforcement night', this was the money shot of Police Operations! This was the night that it all came together and we were going to take down a massive cog in the wheel of the Northwest of England's drugs scene! The briefing began in a more formal than usual way, there were a few faces around that I hadn't seen before, they appeared to be Senior Officers and Field Intelligence Officers (FIO's) who were scrambling around with mobile phones and laptops, they looked busy, I wasn't surprised either, the force had put a leave ban in place and cancelled all rest days for frontline Officers. The operation was huge and involved hundreds of officers from all departments across the force, they needed these numbers as 'Monroe's' had the capacity for two to three hundred clubbers, all of whom were potential prisoners. Briefings were being held across other locations too, the plan was to be that Bish and I were to deploy into the club, make a purchase of drugs if possible and wait for the club to fill up, they wanted it full, they wanted a big bang for their buck! Lancashire Police wanted to send a loud message out that they wouldn't tolerate drug dealing scum in their towns and villages, I was impressed, they had everyone onboard; Traffic Officers were out as cut offs to detain any fleeing motorists and to seize any unsafe vehicles, The Police Helicopter Unit were the eyes in the sky, they were to use their 'Night Sun' spot lights to light up the sports field around the venue in case of any 'runners', Vans crammed with 'Riot' Police were to deploy around the venue and create a ring of steel. On top of this, and as a cherry on the cake, entry was to be gained on our signal, by 40 officers who were crammed in the back of a delivery van. They were to be driven up to the venue in an unmarked delivery van which was to be reversed towards the front doors of the club, the van was going to stop and at that point and the 'Riot' Cops were to 'bomb burst' out of the van and through the front entrance of the club. Speed Aggression and Surprise was key to their success, anyone who got in their way was going to get flattened by a riot shield to the face or a baton strike to the body, this was the only way to dominate and contain so many people at once!

The DI introduced us to one of the Public Order Officers who was going to be one of the first through the door, his name was 'Charlie' he towered over us in his blue overalls and greeted us with a smile,

"So, all this stuff is your fault, is it?"

he nodded his head towards the FIO's and Senior Officers. 'Charlie' was an old school cop who had been with the force's tactical unit for years, he looked fit and lean but by the looks of his craggy face and thinning grey hair he was counting down the days till his pension. 'Charlie' had one job to do tonight, 'Charlie' was to enter the club with another Officer when the initial 'Raid' had taken control of the club, he was to locate us, arrest us and put us in handcuffs, we were then to be taken out like we were prisoners and taken to a waiting vehicle. The plan was set, enforcement phase was a 'GO!'

It was pissing down with rain outside, but inside 'Monroe's' it was warming up nicely, it was getting on for about 01:00hrs by now. 'Blondie' hadn't shown up, this concerned me, had he seen something, or had someone from the local Police tipped him off? Either way we had still 'scored' some pills off a fat kid who was dishing 'pills' out like smarties, it was literally like taking candy off a baby. I felt a knot of apprehension in my stomach as I sent my first update by text message to the DI,

'About 100 people',

I waited for a reply…

'Not yet, not enough',

holy shit, this guy really wanted to make a big bang and take a good supply of prisoners tonight I thought.

02:00hrs… 'about 200 now'…

02:10hrs…'Standby, Standby, we're coming!'

I looked at Bish and showed him the message on my phone, he had the look of the Devil in his eyes and grinned like a Cheshire cat,

"WE HAD BETTER GET SOMEWHERE SAFE, YOU KNOW WHATS COMING"

I agreed and we shuffled off to the corner of a seating area by the front doors.

I don't know what I was expecting but I began to get restless after 20 minutes of waiting, this was my way of dealing with the anticipation of what was going to be one of the biggest enforcement actions I was ever going to be involved in. For the tenth time in a minute I looked at the time on my phone, I was restless and the pressure of anticipation was building up, I looked at Bish and barked

"Where the fuck are t…"

I never got to finish my sentence, I was disturbed in mid moan by the sight of a Doorman flying through the air and smashing against the wall of the club, followed by another and another…

A 'Tornado' of riot cops blasted their way through the entrance smashing shields and batons against anything that got in their way. they were 'dominating' the ground and putting everyone into a panic state, most people usually comply when put in this mode, some tried to fight, but they were cut down like daisy's and thrown into the pit of bodies that didn't move out of the way fast enough, this pit of bodies was now growing on the dance floor as the Cops flushed the clubbers out of all the nooks and crannies of the Club. I believed that we were safe in the seated area but this belief was soon proven wrong, a wave of Cops moved swiftly into the 'Booth's' and began to sweep the occupants out towards the dance floor. First it was a hot blinding light in my eyes from a 'Dragon lamp', aptly named due to its strong beam that is as hot as fire and designed to light up outside areas, the heat and strong light temporarily blinded me. I then felt the painful edge of an 'Armadillo' shield that was 'jabbed' into my upper left arm, these are the rectangular shields made of 4mm thick transparent polycarbonate plastic, these rigid shields can be interlocked to form defensive and offensive barriers, similar tactics are used to those of the ancient Roman Armies who interlocked their shields to make impenetrable 'Armadillo' defences when attacked. The shields can also cause considerable pain when used in a downward 'Chopping' motion against the human body, it's called 'shield work' and its very effective at getting people moving. This was a team of officer's who had been trained in the aforementioned 'Chopping' technique, the pain bit into my upper arm, it was similar to that of the worst dead arm that you have ever been given, it definitely motivates you to move. As if I didn't need more motivation, the cops persisted, the shields buffered against me and the 'Arnold Batons' belted into my torso as I fled, I was laughing like a man possessed, the adrenaline was coursing through my veins at a hundred miles an hour, I was in pain and being beaten by the cops, I was enjoying it, it wasn't real pain, I was going to feel the bumps and bruises later, but this was the 'crescendo' of the operation, the end of weeks of stressful undercover investigations and a pressure release like no other. I was tempted to fulfill my role as a 'pill head' and fight back, I didn't, I would have been battered and it served no purpose, I just ran towards the growing pit of bodies screaming and laughing like a crazed 'Hyena'.

The music was off, but my ears were still ringing from it, the lights had been turned up and the brightness from them exposed what a grubby dump 'Monroe's' really was, it was the ultimate 'Catfish' of clubs, shabby décor and peeling paint masked by darkness, flashing lights and a few pretty girls dancing on a stage. Myself, Bish and around 200 clubbers were crammed onto the dance floor when the Commander of the Police Operation stood in front of us and announced that we were all being detained for the purposes of a drugs search, one girl from the crowd obviously didn't get what was happening and shouted from the crowd,

"WHEN YOU ARE FINISHED CAN WE HAVE THE MUSIC BACK ON PLEASE?"

The commander was taken aback by this naïve question momentarily, he shook his head whilst hiding a cheeky grin,

"**No, the club is being closed down, you will all have to leave!**"

The crowd then, as one, let out a 'groan' of despair and disappointment, I empathized with them, they were just kids wanting a good time, some probably didn't do drugs, this was just their scene, and we had closed it down and ruined their night. However, my days of having survivor guilt were long behind me, I had a job to do, I was there to keep these kids safe from Organised Crime Groups who sold death in the shape of a pill.

On cue 'Charlie' and his mate broke ranks and made towards Bish and I, we had made our way to the front of the crowd to make things easier for them. Charlie took hold of me, turned me around and placed me in handcuffs, hands back-to-back, then he double locked the cuffs so that they didn't tighten up, he knew what he was doing and there was an air of confidence in him that you only get from years of experience, 'Charlie' then uttered the immortal words,

"**You are under arrest for being concerned in the supply of controlled drugs!**"

'Charlie' tipped me forward slightly, Bish and I were then led out in front of the crowd,

"**who the fuck are they?**", "**Ay up bad boys**", "**fuck the Police!**" the crowd were getting a bit angry now, I heard shouts of support from behind as we were led past rows on Police Officers dressed in dark blue fireproof riot coveralls, these were the search teams that were now going to search, and if required, arrest every person in the club, they were also going to strip the club looking for evidence of drugs and any license breaches.

The cold air bit into me through my thin T shirt as we went outside, it had been raining and the blue strobe lights from the Police vehicles bounced off the puddles. 'Riot Cops' hustled and bustled around escorting detainees to the especially adapted prisoner lorry, they tried to get hold of us but 'Charlie' swerved them and took us to one side where we awaited our own transport back to be debriefed, we had a long night ahead of us, there was no glamourous 'James Bond' ending. It was paperwork time; Pocket books needed filling in, evidence handed in, statements written, I finally left the office at about 7am and still had a drive back to the Midlands to contend with, I was knackered, but it was worth it. Operation Escort had been a success; Up to 200 people were searched in the club, seven people were arrested on the night on suspicion of offences including drug possession and possessing offensive weapons. On searching the premises Officers found large quantities of Ecstasy, Amphetamine and Cannabis, these were hidden as I recall near to the front entrance and protected by the door staff. The door staff obviously took their job seriously and also had a selection of weapons at hand too, including two 'tear gas' cannisters and two Samurai swords. 'Blondie' was later arrested for being concerned in the supply of class A drugs; without the DNA evidence we would have never known who he was.

The owner of 'Monroe's' escaped being convicted of being concerned in the supply of drugs and allowing his premises to be used for taking drugs, to be fair to him he was getting on a bit and I think he was being taken advantage of by Organised criminals. The club closed down and failed to rebuild itself to anything more than a wreck of a building, many years later a car was driven into it and it burnt to the ground, 'Monroe's' was finally closed for business.

But, that all aside, drugs are fun!

ENTER THE DRAGON!

(Going to Wales!)

It was early February 2004 when I received another call from the Special Operations Team. I had been a Test Purchaser for around 3 years by now and they wanted someone with my skill set to infiltrate a drugs network in South Wales that were trafficking and dealing in Cocaine! The skill set that I refer to was explained to me by my 'cover officer' in his thick West Midlands accent,
"We need someone who's a cocky little shit and can handle himself if things get tasty, we think 'yam perfick' for the job."

By this time, I had already proven that I was able to work in high-risk arenas like Birmingham with the Yardies, and I had also done a few club jobs so I wasn't a stranger to buying Cocaine and pills. I like to think of myself as confident, but confidence can sometimes make others feel insecure, especially if they lack it or see you as a threat to their 'Alpha' status, so they label you as being cocky in an attempt to put you back in your place!

I agreed to the deployment and promptly told the wife the standard cover story,
"I'm being deployed, it's up north buying Heroin", I lied.

By this time, the wife was getting sick of these deployments and the long hours I worked in my day job. Even more so when I told her it would be 3 months away with me home only a couple days a week, I earned good money which paid for holidays and nice things for the home but this compensating for my absence with material things was beginning to wear thin. I decided that after this job I would concentrate on my growing family and my career, my son was nearly 5 and my daughter had been born just a few months earlier and was still a babe in arms, they needed their dad to be around to help raise them and not be an absent father who is just home a few days a month. Undercover operatives have a shelf life for this exact reason and maybe it was my time to move on. I had completed both my Detectives exam and my Sergeants exam the year before, so there would be other opportunities to concentrate on… If this was going to be my last job, I would make it a good one!

Myself and my new partner in crime called 'Carl' travelled down to meet the Operational Team in a shared hire car. Hire cars are good, we could just dump it if we were compromised and there are no receipts, letters, or any number of other pieces of crap we leave in our own cars that may identify us or our families. They were usually large powerful 2litre engine saloons too, so if needed we could get our foot down and make some distance if we thought we were being followed. The car would have been hired through a company that couldn't be traced back to the Police, this would prevent a nosey or corrupt Police Officer from accessing any information that could compromise the operation or our identity. There was also the risk that someone from an organized crime group knew someone who worked for DVLA in nearby Swansea, or for the national car hire company who could access their computers and see who had hired the car.

The journey was going to take about 3 hours so we decided to use this time to get to know each other and build a cover story for why we were in South Wales and how we knew each other. Carl and I were both white and of a similar age in our early 30's so we didn't look out of place together, Carl was a 'Cockney' and very laddish in his manner, he even called himself a 'Cockney Geezer'. With his shaven head, pointy features, and intense blue eyes he oozed a quiet confidence that I liked and thought was quite reassuring to have. I was confident that the cover officer had also told him that they needed a 'cocky little shit' that could handle himself.

Our cover story had already been partially put together for us; we were being supplied a beaten up old white Ford Transit van that had been salvaged from the crusher after coming to the end of its useful life. We were to be laborer's who were looking for 'cash in hand' work, the economy in Cardiff had exploded and there was a lot of building work in the city at this time, including the new devolved parliament building. Although our cover story was based in Cardiff our targets were not, just across the other side of the bay was a small up and coming town that was beginning to feel the benefits of the region's financial growth.

Penarth was a Victorian Seaside town that was full of character, it had a high street that was lined with Cafés, bars and boutique shops, there were nice parks and beach areas that families could visit for days out. House prices were on the rise as young professionals sort a beachfront refuge away from the hustle and bustle of city life, and commuters from Penarth could sip their posh coffees and warm their hands on their insulated cups whilst catching the ferry across the bay to go to their office jobs in the vibrant Welsh capital city. This kind of money will always attract business, and that business includes drugs like Cocaine! There is also always a keen following of local entrepreneurs with readymade criminal networks who want to get in on the action!

***

"Right then boys, we're going to do this job by the book and there's no rush and no pressure for quick results", The Detective Inspector (DI), snapped out in a sharp South Wales accent. The teams Detective Sergeant (DS) followed this up with **"We have at least three months to get into the local network and we don't want to fuck it up by rushing"**.

I liked the sound of this team already, Undercover test purchase operations used to only last a couple weeks and there was always a rush to maximize opportunities for arrests and big news headlines! A good operation and a positive media piece in the regional newspapers could be the ticket for someone's promotion. This was at times done at the expense of our safety and the people targeted were usually low-level users caught up in the 'dragnet'.

The DI and DS were both local men, the DI was a very serious character with a smart clipped moustache and thinning black hair. He had a day job as an area Detective Inspector, so had other commitments beyond us, he was always smartly dressed and in and out of our location for meetings, but he made the effort to be with us as much as he could to ensure we had our pre deployment briefings. The DS was a scruffy little man with a strong local accent, and like most Detective Sergeants he was a bit rough around the edges and you could have a laugh with him. He spent the most time with us, and he looked after the cover team that was there in case things went wrong. Both had one thing in common though, they were committed to making sure we were looked after.

***

Like builders and workers across the world do every week, we thought that our first Friday should start with some afternoon beers. We had sourced some work clothes and fluorescent bibs and I still had my work boots from my brick factory days, to complete the look we had dirty white hard hats too. We had been given very little information about targets or what pubs to go in on purpose, **"Just go and have a few beer's lads and see who pops up, I want to test our intelligence"** said the DI in a matter-of-fact way that put me at ease… Ok, free beers it is I thought!

Obviously, we couldn't get pissed up every time we went out, and thankfully we had the van as an excuse if one of us wasn't drinking. We had to find a bar with a Pool table, this would slow down the consumption of alcohol and they have an added benefit too! Pool tables are a magnet for young at heart drinkers, these are the well-paid builders, the degenerates and the up-and-coming drug dealers who feed off of them; these people would be our doorway into the local drugs scene! Without a doubt Wales is a friendly place and everyone made us feel welcome, in no time we had struck up a conversation with some of the drinkers in one of the High Street chain pubs, our cover story stood up and we talked about the rugby world cup that was on at the time and good places to eat and drink. We asked about pool tables, it's rare to find a pool table in a chain pub, their venues are for food and drinks. They are quite clever about maximizing their space and don't want the place clogged up with the local idiots fighting over a pool table. That's another thing about pool tables, they're a flash point for violence and pool cues become weapons, especially if the locals think outsiders are trying to muscle in on their territory, we had to make sure we lost a few games, just so as not to make any enemies. One of our new friends said that the best pubs for Pool tables were 'The Queens', 'The Harbour' and 'The Blacksmiths'… **"Actually boys, we're off to 'the Blacksmiths' now, they do a good pint, fancy coming?"** We accepted this kind offer. Walking into a pub as strangers can bring some negative attention, any good criminal would know you are strangers and their hackles of suspicion would be triggered! But walking in with local people as their friends is a good reference and takes some of the suspicion and anxiety out of our presence, the least we could do was buy our new mate a beer when we got there.

We parted company from our new friend telling him we were off to play pool, he was a civilian and to my knowledge nothing to do with the local drugs network. I didn't want to drag him into our investigation if I didn't have to, however if he threw himself on the sword at a later date and it was apparent he was involved then he would become a legitimate target! I was not in the business of setting people up to commit crimes, nor was I in the business of making a guy, who had just been friendly, a scape goat who could get a beating or worse for introducing undercover Police Officers as his friends.

The 'Blacksmiths Arms' was an old-fashioned pub situated in a row of terrace houses, from the front it looked no bigger than the other houses on the street. There was a small seating area to the front where you could sit in the sun smoking and watch the world go by, Inside the pub had the smell of beer and cigarettes that is loved and replicated the world over. The bar was to the right and ran half the length of the building to the back of the pub where it opened up to a larger area, this was where the pool table was situated. Carl was trying to get to the bar to buy some beers, there were only a few locals at the bar so I knew it wouldn't take long for him to be served. **"Grab some change for the pool table"** I half shouted to him **"I'm just off for a piss"** ... I lied; I was going for a reconnaissance! where were the fire exits? was there a back door? who was in the bar? were there any obvious threats to our safety? The pub had a strange layout, to get to the toilets you had to go down a spiral staircase where I also found of all things a bowling alley. I had found the fire exits and I was happy there were no threats, so I returned to the pool table for a well earnt pint of cold lager!

It didn't take long for the magnetic pull of the pool table to produce its first degenerate, **"Hello boys, not seen you around here before"** a young skinny lad said in a strong Welsh accent as he placed 20p on the side of the table, this is the international sign that he wanted to pay for the next game and play the winner. **"Just in the area for work mate, wanted somewhere out of town where we could chill and play some pool"** the conversation went on... **"where's good to go out around here, y'know, where's good to party?"**

This skinny white lad called 'Sidney' was barely 16 years old and was desperately trying to be our new mate. Sidney told us there was a club in the town on the high street or we could go to Cardiff where there are loads of 'birds' and better clubs, then out of the blue, he offered **"Do you boys want to buy some weed?"** I was slightly taken a back at this as he had only just met us, he was so young and reckless that I actually felt sorry for him and thought I shall give him a free pass. **"Nah not really mate, I do weed sometimes but I'm more into the coke and pills scene"** I leant forward and took another shot at the black ball which had been hovering over a pocket.

"Oh, you'll be ok then, there's a few boys around here who can sort you out, you sure you don't want some weed?" His response made me miss my shot and the white ball clattered around the table.

Fuck it I thought, this kid is throwing himself on the sword, we will use him to gain some credibility. **"Fuck it, go on then, I'll have a 20 bag"** indicating that I wanted £20 worth, Sidney scurried off and returned after 5 minutes with a small stash of Cannabis in clingfilm, it looked like he had just swept the insides of a tea bag off the floor and wrapped it in clingfilm, I had no confidence that this would be quality gear!… I slipped him his £20 and placed the weed in my pocket. Sidney was our first contact but I had no intention of buying off him again, he was a drippy kid and of no consequence in the bigger picture. However, people in the bar had seen us with him and had seen me buying the 'weed', if asked Sidney would say we were 'cool' and that we had bought weed off of him, that was the aim.

We headed back to our safe location for a debrief and to hand over the evidence from the deployment. The DS was ecstatic with excitement! The 'Blacksmiths' was now on the list of locations of interest and in that short time we had established local contacts, purchased drugs and had had our faces seen in the pub. We were to redeploy the next night and try some other locations in the town.

One of the operational team took us to our accommodation in a nearby seaside town, I winced as he proudly presented us a rundown B&B that was over a local pub! The rooms were damp and looked like they were last decorated in World War 2, the shower was down the hallway and you could hear and smell the pub below, I was not happy! The next day I went straight into see the DS,

"The accommodation is not suitable! It's a fucking shit hole over a pub!"

he was taken aback by my comment and asked why?

"You don't put undercovers into shitty local pub accommodation! People talk to you and want to get to know you... its full of degenerates and the place is a shit hole!"

It wasn't their fault, the team thought we would like a place where we could have a pint and relax. We had no cover officer on the ground to offer them guidance and to look after our welfare. This went against procedure but 'Special Operations' had run out of cover officers so The Ds had offered to do it on top of his operational work... this façade of looking after us was worrying me, their lack of experience wasn't their fault but putting us in a pub B&B was a dangerous mistake, they were devastated at this and promised to get us moved ASAP!

Buying drugs in Penarth wasn't easy, we had to get our faces known about the town and break through the suspicions of people who had lived in this community their whole life. They had close family and relatives around them and people they went to school with, we stood out as outsiders and on top of that we were English! In some parts of Wales, they dislike us with a nationalistic passion that goes back hundreds of years, you can walk into a pub and people will stop talking English and switch to their native Welsh language. I realized that this was still alive and well when I cheered an England win against Wales in the rugby. The looks across the bar made me realize it was time to make a quick exit and try another bar, I suppose it could have added to our cover to be just two lads celebrating a sports win for our country, it was natural behaviors, but we were there to infiltrate and buy drugs, not get involved in bar fights!

Carl was getting jumpy, we were struggling to get into any of the dealers and he was desperate to score some cocaine, I felt like he wanted to prove something to the operational team at any cost. He was also starting to irritate me! his voice would go through me like nails down a chalk board every time he started with his 'Cockney Geezer' act. These tight knit communities are very friendly, until you annoy them! In these parts they have no problem with sorting out disputes with a punch to the mouth and with us being outsiders we could soon find the whole pub queueing up to take a swing at us.

We had quite a few bars to choose from so we chose the 'Harbour', as you can imagine it wasn't far from the Harbour by its name and as an added bonus it had the obligatory pool tables! As we walked in, we saw a group of about 8 lads, all were in their late twenties and dressed quite well with designer clothing and smart haircuts. These could have been any group of lads you see out on the town, so we thought they would be good to chat to. A nod of the head and an **"Alright mate?"** was reciprocated with **"Alright Butt, how's it going?"** from one of the crowd, the ice was broken,

"You lads off out on the town tonight then?" I asked

"Oooh just a few with the lads you know, we don't get out as much as before, kids and that, you know" Came his reply in a soft and friendly local accent.

Ok I thought, let's see if they throw themselves on the sword or are they just good people out enjoying a pint with their friends. 'Cockney Geezer' was over to my right and starting his routine, I carried on talking to my new mate about why we were in town and general chat, it was way too early to be tapping him up for drugs or a number of a dealer.

"Fuck Me Lads!!! Gonna have to watch these boys I reckon they're coppers!!!"

My head snapped to the right in the direction of the words, a deep pain in my stomach clenched to fight back the nerves and stop any overt reaction to this allegation. This is the moment of make or break in a situation like this, had we been compromised? Where was the nearest exit? Fuck !!! it was crowded so we would have to fight our way out!!! The only other exit was at the far end of the bar and running the gauntlet through a whole pub would get messy. What had happened? Carl was stood there in the middle of a huddle of the group looking as shocked as I felt. I'm sure that if I had looked in a mirror, I would have looked like a rabbit in the headlights too. I soon worked out what had happened, 'Cockney Geezer' had come to life and mixed with his desperation to be the first to buy drugs, he had pushed things too fast and gone in for the kill!

"Look mate, we don't do that stuff, just drink your beer and enjoy your night" stated one of the group, I guessed it was the same guy that had said we were 'coppers'. Carl looked angry and appeared to stand there momentarily sulking, He shook it off and returned to character but I could see he was looking at me. I had moved slightly away from the group with the guy I was talking to and thought it best to disengage a bit, play pool with this lad and pretend I had never heard what was said.

"We're leaving!" it was the same guy from the bar, he was speaking to the lad I was playing pool with!

"What's up?" he asked

"Just come now!"

My pool buddy looked bewildered but began to follow his mate out the bar.

I looked over at carl who was stood nonchalantly at the bar with his pint,

"What's happened, you reckon they're onto us" I asked?

"I sorted it mate" he said with a cocky grin on his face,

"Sorted what, what's happened" I asked?

"I followed that bloke into the toilets and fronted him out for calling me a copper! I told him if he said that to someone in London, he would get stabbed"

My jaw dropped open and I could feel the blood leaving my face, I was exasperated at this disaster!

"You can't go around threatening to stab people, they could be on their way back with mates to give us a kicking, we need to leave" I put my pint down and Carl followed me out of the bar.

Back at the debrief Carl retold his story and I made my representations that it probably wasn't the best of moves but that I understood why he had done it. I was lying, I kept my views as low key as I could, I didn't want the boss to kick us off the job for this mistake. At the end of the day Carl was my partner and although he was annoying me, we had to look out for each other, I thought we could work these issues out like adults.

I had always been taught that honest feedback is key to building a good team, I was subjected to this numerous times both in the Army and the Police, you get to hear some harsh truths, and it can hurt, but that honest feedback is key to the growth of you as an operator and to the success of the team. I had to start it somewhere so I started on the way back to our accommodation, I explained my concerns about what had happened that night and how communities like this stick together, we could have a whole family gunning for us and wouldn't be safe in any of the pubs in town. He said nothing and just looked forward... We were outsiders and if we didn't tow the line we would compromise the job and probably get a kicking. He just sat there glowering in a deep mood and stared out of the car window, I could see he wasn't happy!

"Look Carl, I'm no expert at all this, and from what you've told me you've done more jobs than me so I'm happy to take some feedback off you if you think I'm going wrong" I offered as an olive branch of reconciliation.

No reply came, he just sat there staring out of the window with anger bubbling beneath the surface. It was time to just leave him with his thoughts, I had said my piece and I had given him the chance to come back at me, it was time to let him take it on board and calm down.

***

The next day we returned to town and made our way to the 'Blacksmiths', Carl was still brooding so I decided to give him a wide berth and try and forget last night's episode. Carl was a good operator and got on with the job at hand, he stayed at the bar and chatted to a couple of the locals, I went to the pool table and began playing against one of the local lads. It was a Thursday and the bar was not too busy with around 10 to 20 people in there, but it was quite lively with the sound of laughter and music from the Jukebox which made it a nice atmosphere. There was one woman near to the bar who was quite attractive; blonde hair and dressed seductively in a leopard print top that showed her cleavage, she had the black mini skirt on and high heels to finish the look off. This woman was alone and very drunk, she was making her way around the bar leaning up against the men and being overly friendly. Some of the men in the bar seemed happy with this, others, who were with wives and girlfriends were not.

"Come with me"

Carl had come from the bar and as soon as he had said it walked off, I wasn't sure what he had said and leant down to take another shot.

Carl returned "I NEED YOU TO COME WITH ME NOW!!!"

"Yeah, OK let me just take this shot" I calmly replied

"NO NOW!!!" ordered Carl in a louder and more determined voice, I could see that something was up and without hesitation I put down the cue and followed him out of the bar. We walked at a fast pace away from the pub and a few streets later I stopped Carl and asked what was up? At this he exploded,

"WHEN I SAY WE FACKING LEAVE, WE FACKING LEAVE! IT WAS ABOUT TO KICK OFF IN THERE AND THINGS COULD HAVE GOT NASTY"

I was confused,

"What are you on about, what had we done, are we compromised?" I asked.

Carl was still shouting, "NO, THAT FACKING WOMAN IN THERE, THE LOCALS THOUGHT SHE WAS A COPPER AND THEY WERE GOING TO GIVE HER A FACKING BEATING, ONE OF THE WOMEN SAID SHE KNEW HER AND THAT SHE WAS IN THERE TRYING TO GET INFORMATION"

"So, we left for that? They're probably more pissed off that she's flirting with their men" I replied.

At that Carl exploded again,

"I'VE HAVE HAD A FACKING NUFF OF YOU, YOU BOTTLED IT LAST NIGHT AND SHOULD HAVE BACKED ME UP, I COULD SEE YOU WERE SHITTING YOURSELF!"

I was taken aback…he was raging at me, there was a place for feedback and I was happy to take it in the debrief, but not on a terrace street in the middle of Penarth! I held my hands up to my front with my palms outstretched indicating him to 'calm down' and in a slow voice I said,

"Mate you need to calm down, we nearly got compromised last night because of you trying too hard! yeah I was scared, you gotta trust me I had your back, but you don't go around threatening to stab people!" "And can I remind you of what you are and where you are right now! You need to stop shouting and calm the fuck down before someone hears you and we are compromised!"

My mobile phone burst into life, it was the DS, he told us that the team were extracting us and that we were to meet them nearby, I cannot go into the technicalities of how or why but our cover team had been able to monitor this whole conversation as it unfolded. We bundled ourselves into the back of the unmarked police car and headed out of town for a debrief.

The DI was at the debrief, he didn't look happy, he had the look of a school master who was about to administer the cane to a pair of naughty pupils. I wasn't overly worried, in my mind I knew that I hadn't done anything wrong, but they could pull the whole job and replace us if they had wanted. We had been there a few weeks and had only made a couple of low-level drugs purchases, were we going wrong somewhere or was their intelligence wrong? Was the drugs scene in Penarth not as bad as they thought, the pressure of not making any progress was starting to put a lot of stress on all of us.

"Right boys, I can't have a repeat of what just happened again! I am going to have to report it back to Special Operations and I'm sure the DCI there will want to talk to you about it"

This was bad, I was pretty new to this game compared to Carl and I thought his seniority would out trump me if they had to choose who to pull from the job. This was potentially my last undercover deployment and I didn't want it to end with me being returned to normal duties, I had to make this work!

"Now, can I trust you two to get on with each other for the next few days?"

We both nodded like naughty school kids, it was time to be professionals and our egos had to take second place if this was going to be a successful operation…

SLAYING THE DRAGON

(Evidence and Enforcement)

LUCK OF THE IRISH

We had been deploying to the town for the past month and barely scraped together any decent product or any decent suspects. Carl and I had fallen out and a lot of that was to do with both of us being Alpha characters and wanting to be seen to be the top operator who was producing evidence and results. We had both been recruited to this job because we could handle confrontation and neither of us was going to be the other one's number two. We had to get on with the job at hand so we agreed to make it work for the sake of the operation, this was to become a full-time acting job where we had to tolerate each other and put our differences aside. Perhaps we needed that fall out? Teams that come together have a period of 'storming,' 'norming' and 'forming'! This is an accepted team building process where people who have never worked together are forced into doing so, and as a result of the storming and norming they find their natural pecking order and form a productive team that can work together and deliver results.

St Patrick's Day was a turning point for the investigation, I thought 'fuck this, I'm going for it tonight!' I had chatted to a few local faces over the past weeks and tonight I was going to 'drop it on someone's toes' and just ask if they could hook me up.

We were back in the 'chain pub' that evening and we bought a couple of pints, it was a busy night, it was a Wednesday and St Patrick's Day! A great excuse to get on the beer, even if we were in Wales and not Ireland, the day has become an international excuse to drink Guinness and sing along to music by the 'Pogues.'

"Hi Mate, how's it going, I don't suppose you could help me out could you?" I asked one of the lads I had met a few nights before,

"Hello Butt, what's occurring?" came back a very Welsh answer,

"I wanna score some 'Coke,' y'know a bit of 'Charlie,' I hate to ask but we don't know anyone around here"

"OH, you want to nip down the 'Queens' butt, ask for 'Donny,' you'll see him, he looks special," to reinforce the point he made his face and hands screw up like he had some kind of disability. I had to laugh at this as he nearly fell over as he tensed up his whole body to make his point. There is no place for sensitivity or political correctness in undercover work, it may be something that is expected in the normal workplace, but on the streets and within criminal networks it doesn't mean anything! Being offended or challenging someone about an inappropriate comment can get you a beating or worse.

"Tell him Baz sent you down" he kindly added…

The Queens was pretty deserted except for a small huddle of around four blokes in the corner, they looked tired and craggy, their worn-out clothes and battered middle aged faces told a story of a lifetime of hard drinking and wasted potential. They lived the pub life because there was nothing to go home to except an empty bedsit or a nagging wife, their benefits were spent in the pub, and if any other opportunities like petty crime came up to make a few quid, they'd take it and repeat the cycle of alcohol dependance.

We racked up the pool table and bought a couple of pints, the landlady was really friendly and offered me a couple of oversized St Patrick's Day top hats that the brewery had sent out to add to the party spirit, they looked like large pints of Guinness with a green hat rim around the base to make it look like a leprechaun's top hat. So, there we were, two undercover cops on St Patrick's Day 2004 being the life of the party with 'fairy tale of New York' blasting out of the Jukebox in a deserted pub in South Wales. What a pair of twats we must have looked whilst we played pool in our new headgear, it bought a few smiles from the old fellas in the corner and the Landlady seemed pleased to have some action in the bar.

The bar door swung open and a young guy in his twenties strolled in, he looked like he had just finished work on a building site, he was wearing the standard Florescent Jacket, jeans, and boots of a builder. He was very similar looking to Carl with his shaven head and sharp features, Was this 'Donny'? Carl was stood at the slot machine which he was slowly filling up at the expense of the Taxpayer, **"What do you reckon, do you think its him?"** I asked…

"Could be, no one else is here, might be worth a go" Carl replied.

The builder had joined the huddle of old timers in the corner and they huddled in together as thick as thieves.

"Fuck it, hold my pint!" I whispered to Carl…

"Excuse me lads" I crouched at the end of the table where the huddle was sitting, I looked at the builder and asked, **"Are you Donny mate, wondered if you could help me out?"**

"NO, I'm Donny, whose fucking asking?" came a sharp reply from the guy sat next to him in the corner, his voice was raspy and rough like that of an old smoker, obviously another habit that he had picked up along the way. This aggressive reply momentarily took me aback, but I quickly recovered,

"Sorry mate, I'm not trying to get in anyone's face, I'm just trying to score some Charlie, a lad called Baz up the 'spoons' said

to ask for Donny," I remained passive and nonconfrontational as I looked up at the craggy old face of my challenger.

"**Well Baz wants to keep his fucking mouth shut, now go back to your game**" he ordered!

I felt dejected as I stood up and my shoulders drooped in defeat as I paced across the bar, I looked up and saw a big grin on Carl's face and realized I also looked ridiculous with the stupid Leprechaun hat on too. We huddled by the slot machine pissing ourselves laughing and I began to waste some more Taxpayer's money whilst we tried to control our laughter.

A couple of minutes later the builder, who I shall now refer to as 'BOB' for ease of reading came over to us, he edged up next to me and asked,

"**How much Charlie do you want mate?**"

"**A gram will do, we're off to the city soon and want to get some before we go**" I replied thinking a gram wasn't too much to ask for.

"**OK 60 quid**"

I took the cash from my pocket and surreptitiously passed it to him concealing the transaction from the Landlady. 'BOB' slipped the notes into his pocket and palmed me a wrap of foil which I placed in my pocket. 'BOB' then returned to his band of merry men and joined the huddle in the corner. I felt kind of sorry for the Landlady at the pub, it was what was supposed to be a busy night with plenty of people spending money on drinks and having a laugh. But all she was stuck with was this band of degenerates nursing a pint for an hour at a time and selling class A drugs under her nose. 'BOB' was acting as a runner for Donny, obviously he still didn't trust us, maybe he thought we were cops? Sending his runner across to us was a good idea, by doing this he had passed all the risk to BOB who could have been arrested by us there and then. We now needed to make our excuses and leave, 'BOB' was a total user and was hanging around like a bad smell and was trying to tap us up for a line of coke, we didn't want to crack open the evidence and lose half the product or be put in a position where we were expected to start doing lines.

This was a turning point for the operation, and more importantly for mine and carl's relationship. We had stepped up to the mark and delivered our first real purchase of 'coke,' we now had a target to focus on and a location from which to build a picture of the local drugs scene. I even received a pat on the shoulder from carl, a cheeky wink and a "**Nice one Geezer, that was good work tonight.**"

***

We left the pub and headed into the town to get a Taxi into Cardiff where we were going to be picked up. By some twist of fate Carl struck up a conversation with a friendly Taxi driver who was taking our fare to Cardiff, he was sat in the front and I was sat in the back leaning forward between the front seats,

"**Busy night mate?**" the standard Taxi conversation began…I was glad to be sat in the back

"**What time you finish?**" … it went on.

Taxi man, who now told us he was called 'Jake' was really chatty, too chatty, like he was on something, I didn't mind, it was an effective way of testing our cover story. "**So, you boys off into town to get some birds and do some coke?**"

I was beginning to see that Cocaine and other drugs were just part of normal conversation in these parts, but coming up with the goods was another matter, Carl had picked up on this too and replied,

"**Yeah mate, we scored some scraps in the pub but it doesn't look that good, hopefully we can get some better gear in the city, we wanna have a fackin party!!!**" Carl was doing his best 'Cockney Geezer' act and it was working!

"**Let's see what you got then boys?**" Jake was older than us and a big set bloke, his request was more of a demand! I opened up the wrap of coke and the cheeky bastard went and dabbed his finger in it and started rubbing it on his gums like he was 'Al Pacino' in 'Scarface.' I snatched it back and wrapped it up… he paused…

"Yeah, that's fucking shit, here's my card, I'm not holding any gear tonight but if you want coke give me a call," He handed carl his taxi card which had his personal number written on it in biro pen.

"Nice one Geezer!" the 'Cockney Geezer' was at it again; I smiled and allowed a little chuckle to myself as his cartoon character emerged right on cue.

***

The next day we decided to try our luck with our new target Jake! He had thrown himself well and truly on the sword. He had offered to supply us Cocaine and had given us his personal mobile phone number, we had his taxi ID number and we had his car registration too. You don't often get a fully identifiable target who is expecting you to call him. This was too good an opportunity to miss!

I called Jake in the late afternoon, he had been out working all night so I didn't want to wake him too early and piss him off or look too desperate,

"Hi mate, Its Jack from last night, you said you can sort us some Charlie?"

I heard him clearing his throat and sparking up a cigarette as he considered his answer

"Aye, Aye, did you boys have a good night in town?" his friendly question surprised me so I told him we had pulled a couple girls and that the night went well.

To my surprise Jake then offered,

"I'll meet you at the Blacksmiths about 7 tonight, £50 for a gram, will that do you?"

"You couldn't make it 2 grams could ya?" I cheekily asked, without a pause he agreed.

It was on!!! There was a buzz of excitement in the team, this was the moment they had been waiting for! Their intelligence gathering and their hard planning was starting to bear fruit. We were lucky, we had the sexy job of playing the poor man's James Bond. These guys were what made the magic happen, they spent hours in observation vehicles where they pissed in bottles and in extreme circumstance's crapped into clingfilm if they couldn't hold nature back. They did this to gather important evidential video footage of our interactions with our targets, they were also our personal bodyguards If the shit hit the fan and we had to escape from a confrontation! On our signal these guys would run in and rain hell down on whoever showed the slightest inkling of aggression, it was comforting to know they were there in the shadows. We also had an Officer in the Case (OIC) who took charge of the case building, they gathered all of our statements, pocketbooks and video evidence as well as managing all the drugs exhibits for court. This is to name but a few people that help run the whole operation, and It's easy to forget you are part of a bigger team when you are out there on the streets acting as a drug user to gather evidence. Without all these unsung heroes our job was very dangerous and evidentially pointless, it was great to see them so excited about another potential target.

Jake sauntered in late at around half seven, we had got there early and located ourselves at the pool table. Some of the locals were getting used to us being around and we were even offered early 'dibs' on the warm meat pies that the landlady served from behind the bar, in other circumstances this could easily have been my local boozer. I was too wired to eat, so I topped myself up with a cool pint of lager and racked up another game of pool. Jake was talking to another guy by the front doors, after a few nods and handshakes Jake walked towards us through the bar, last time I had seen him he had been sat down in his taxi, but now he was towering over me at over six foot tall. Jake pointed at me and ordered

"**Follow me!**" as he headed down the stairs to the toilets.

I thought this was a fair request as he probably didn't want to deal out in the open. I followed Jake into the brightly lit toilets and was immediately hit by the smell of chlorine and piss from the overflowing urinals on the wet tile floors. I was starting to feel the tightening in my gut as my body prepared itself for the transaction of cash for drugs, it was a flashpoint moment that could go wrong in so many ways. I had to control my nerves as my brain prepared itself for the fight or flight reaction that would come if my cover story went wrong, I could get stabbed, beaten or even kidnapped and tortured... Jake opened up one of the cubicles on the left and went inside, I heard him tapping something onto the porcelain top of the toilet, I then heard two sharp nasal 'Snorts,' the noise that is made when someone inhales Cocaine through their nose. Jake stepped out and in his left hand he held a rolled up £20 note, he handed me the note whilst he gestured into the cubicle and ordered

"**Your turn Boyo!**"

In front of me I saw on top of the toilet cistern two perfectly formed 5cm long white lines of powder, next to it was an open wrap containing more white powder!

'FUCK' this was a test! He was testing to see if I was really an undercover Police Officer, If I didn't hoover up these white lines like a true user I would have been outed as a cop and things would escalate rapidly! I was trapped in this underground toilet with this giant bear of a man, and it wasn't even slightly romantic!

I had to think on my feet but I had no way of making my excuses, this was on and I had to take some kind of action. I took control of my fight or flight instincts and buried them deep inside me, it was not the time to do either. I took the £20 note from Jake and pushed past him slightly knocking into him in a kind of arrogant 'get out the way then' manner. As I leant forward to the cistern Jake towered over me from behind watching what I was doing, I'd never done coke in my life and here I was faced with two lines of Columbia's finest right in front of me. Evidentially and morally, it was wrong for me to 'snort' the coke and in only the direst of situations would I have done it to protect my cover. I have read accounts of undercover Cops snorting coke, smoking weed and even being in drug dens where people are injecting heroin. This may have been acceptable in the past but in the early 2000's this was not tolerated, it puts you in danger of poisoning and compromises your evidence! You should always have an excuse why you cannot take the drugs in front of the target, I didn't, and I was skating on thin ice… I had to make my move!

I heard the door to the toilets crash open which in turn startled Jake, he leant back and closed the door on me whilst he looked out at who had just walked in. This was it! now or never! I quickly brushed my left hand across the cistern causing the two perfect white lines to disappear into a pool of piss and chlorine on the tiled floor. I then made my own two 'Snorting' noises through the £20 note that Jake had earlier given me, this was enough of a distraction to make it look like I had hoovered the lines up like a pro. I handed Jake back his £20 note and took the wrap from the top of the cistern. My nerves were starting to crack however, my hands were shaking as I picked up the open wrap that had been left in the cubicle. I handed it to Jake and asked him to wrap it back up

"Some of that shit has got in my eyes" I explained as I shaked and wiped my face like I had just been hit by a massive dose of Cocaine.

Jake giggled and seemed happy with both my ability to snort coke and the reaction it had taken on me; I had passed the test and I handed Jake the £100 I had in my pocket and he blatantly handed over 2grams of Columbian marching powder. As I walked out of the toilet I was aware of my partner Carl coming down the stairs to use the toilet. I knew what he had been up to, he had been waiting on the stairs near enough to react if there was any commotion downstairs, it was good to know he had my back!

As I recalled my far from romantic toilet liaisons with Jake to the team back at the debrief the adrenaline began to leave my body, I was shaking and hyperactive like I was actually high from the Cocaine. They sat their open mouthed as I bounced around explaining how I had taken the opportunity to discard the cocaine and pretend to snort it, this was beyond what we all had expected to happen. Jake was obviously switched on and we had to watch for further tests, this was to be factored into any further dealings with him and excuses needed to be made so as not to be put in that position again.

We continued to buy from Jake and we arranged to meet him in places where we couldn't be tested, it was annoying him. He turned up in his Taxi to serve up, he even charged us the extra £2 for the taxi fare! After our third deal Jake handed us over to one of his runners, I was obviously annoying him, he had always treated me with an aggressive tone and I don't think there was any love lost between us, he referred to me as a 'Little shit,' I didn't care though, he wanted to be the 'big man' and dominate me, I knew that I would have the last laugh. I was however, not prepared for and shocked by what I was about to be part of. Jake told me to go to the newspaper shop and ask for Cheryl, she would sort me out, he was too busy doing Taxi runs. We found the shop on a side street near to the town center; it was only a small place that fitted between the terrace houses. Inside was a typical local newspaper shop, local papers sat next to the national papers on the floor and there were various magazines on the shelves, a small counter displayed a selection of chocolate and sweets for kids to buy on the way home from school, and there was a cigarette display behind the counter out of reach of the same small hands.

"**Excuse me, can I speak to Cheryl? Jake sent me here to collect something**" I politely asked the old lady behind the counter.

The old lady looked up at me over the top of her metal rimmed spectacles, she could have been my nan, she had wavy light grey hair and a face that was gaunt and wrinkled from ageing, her thin body was hidden under a white blouse and a salmon coloured cardigan. She gave me a friendly smile and reached for her leather handbag

"**Oh, you must be the boys who are coming for the cocaine**" she purred out in a kindly voice,

My jaw nearly hit the floor as this old lady produced a wrap of coke from within her handbag and held it out for me to take.

"**OH, Right, Yeah, Fanks**" was all I managed to blurt out in surprise and embarrassment at what was happening.

So, there I was in a newspaper shop on a back street of a South Wales town buying 2 grams of cocaine from a little old lady who I thought was old enough to be my grandmother. This turn of events took us both by surprise, it just didn't make sense, the main thought that came through my mind was that Jake was taking advantage of a vulnerable person. I already had a low opinion of Jake and this just reinforced to me what a bastard he really was. We never dealt with Jake after this, we had bought enough from him evidentially anyway, Cheryl had thrown herself on the sword so we had no choice but to make her our next target. Carl arranged another couple of purchases with Cheryl, one of which was at her home, it was a proper old person's bungalow on the edge of town in a row of similar council type properties, the outside was clean with small well-tended communal gardens to the front. The inside of the house was clean and had that musty smell of the gas fire mixed with the smell of food cooking on the stove, it was basically your grandmother's house which made this whole experience surreal. Cheryl took us into her living room where we sat on her sofa which was adorned with lace doilies, we ate biscuits and drank tea from delicate floral patterned China cups that she filled from a tea pot she had prepared before we had arrived. I got the feeling she was happy for some company and happily chatted away to us, it turned out she was quite the drug dealer and even offered to ask around for some ecstasy pills from the people she knew. Had we got this the wrong way around? was she controlling Jake? Was she so far out there that she thought drugs were now legal? Questions we would never know the answers to…Carl handed over the cash and was given his wrap of Cocaine. We both walked out of the house in dazed amazement and agreed that this lady must be either living on a different planet or was a relic of the 60's drug culture and was just a drug dealer that had grown old. The whole culture of drugs in this area was bizarre, I was never able to identify what I considered to be a stereotypical drug dealer, they didn't look rich, they had no bling jewelry or designer clothing and most had day jobs too. It appeared to be just something that people were doing to gain some local credibility or earn a couple of quid on the side, none of this made any sense.

SLAYING THE DRAGON

The enforcement phase was a big day for everyone, Carl and I were long gone and our targets would barely remember us being around. We were just those two English dickheads who slept in their van and enjoyed a bit of Charlie. The operational team gathered all the evidence on each individual target, every deal we had made was evidenced with our statements and forensic reports to prove that what we had bought was a controlled drug. There was video evidence, telephone evidence and DNA reports, all of which would be placed into an arrest package with a photo of the suspect, their address and a warrant to allow them rapid entry to secure the premises and the evidence within. Each target of the operation was allocated to an investigation team who simultaneously executed warrants at the home addresses of all targets across the Vale of Glamorgan. Their homes were searched and further evidence like drugs, money and mobile phones were seized to strengthen the case against them. Suspect interviews followed and the local solicitors were inundated with requests to attend 'Barry' Police Station to represent clients, most of who were still in shock after the search teams had destroyed the locks on their front doors and had rudely woken them from their slumber. During the interviews, as expected, there were denials and excuses for why they had drugs in their possession, anything to distance themselves from being concerned in the supply of drugs. The interviews were paused and the solicitors were then given further disclosure of evidence, this evidence identified Carl and I as undercover police officers. The penny dropped and faces turned ashen grey at the realization that those 'two English dickheads' were in fact professional Police evidence gatherers. 'Jake' was heard to say words to the effect" **Jack can't be a copper I saw him snorting coke,"** my statement was read to him detailing how I had avoided this, he was then heard to say words to the effect of **"the Little shit!"**

Carl and I had spent 3 months in what is a lovely part of Wales working with an effective team of dedicated officers, without their help and support we would not have been able to do our jobs. The local people were always friendly and we were often offered accommodation when they heard we were sleeping in our van, this gave me faith in the community and was a true testament to their kind hearts. We had a slow start, but the operation built momentum and we quickly identified various dealers in the town, we had bypassed the lower end of the scale of dealer because we were known to have readily available cash, and money talks. I have only spoken of a few of the deployments on this operation, there were too many to mention or even remember. I have changed the names of those involved in an attempt to protect their identities, but I owe them nothing. They were willing to sell illegal class A drugs and they knew the risks of what they were doing. I had long forgotten the days of survivor guilt I had after my first deployments, my only pity, if you can call it that, was towards the licensees of the bars that were being used to deal from. Their livelihoods had been put at risk by a few degenerates who abused their hospitality and saw no further than making money off the back of a trade that causes misery across the world. Nearly 20 years on I'm sure that some of those I have written about have shrugged off their mortal coil and are no longer of this world, or they are now grandparents trying to live a good life with their families. I hold them no malice and hope that they are enjoying their lives with their families and understand that the deception that was used was my Job, and it was a job that was necessary to protect other people's children and grandchildren from people like them!

***

That was the end of it, my last deployment, I had decided to now try to build some normality for my family. I had secured a job with a source handling unit, they are the guys who dealt with Police informants, this gave me the 'buzz' and it gave me job satisfaction, it was still in the 'covert' world and that made me happy. My career and the opportunity of promotion was ahead of me, I had to leave this life behind, it was a somber feeling, one that I felt forced into and a decision that I knew was ultimately mine to make, but I resented leaving it anyway.

Best job I ever had!

END GAME

April 2020, the world is in the grip of a pandemic known as Covid-19, a respiratory virus which spread easily from person to person and killed millions in its wake. The country closed down, food and basic necessities soon ran out and people had to join long queues outside supermarkets to stock up with what was available. New laws were put in place which restricted the civil liberties of the country, people had to wear face coverings if outside their homes, you were not allowed out on the streets without a reasonable excuse, and gatherings of people from different households were banned! The National Health Service was also tested to its limits, and all but essential medical care was put on hold, this included mine! The back injury I had sustained at the football match had worsened, I was now working as a Detective Sergeant, so office based mostly, this enabled me to be medicated and move around to relieve the breath-taking pain that ran from the base of my spine to the toes on my left leg. I was trying to Soldier on, be the professional and keep the team going through this unprecedented situation with the pandemic…
But it was not working, I was literally dragging my legs out of the car and hobbling across the car park to get into the office, the medication I was on made me drowsy and I was falling asleep at my desk.

However, the straw that broke the camel's back was the British public, even in these desperate times they continued with their selfish behaviours that I had become used to after 22 years as a Police Officer. People with time on their hands continued to report trivial crimes, these included online arguments and name calling, all of which had to investigated, due to this real crimes never got the true attention they deserved. Then to top this off, an ugly side of human nature started to show its head, neighbours were spying on each other! They were reporting minor 'COVID' breaches where families met up when they shouldn't have, a few people were relishing in the power that the new laws and tougher limitations on freedom gave them. They knew that they were able to pick up the phone, report on their neighbours and the Police would arrive and prosecute those that they found. I didn't like it, it reminded me of Nazi snitches in World War 2 and Communist informants in the Cold War Soviet Union that reported their neighbours for minor infractions, or for disagreeing with a party policy... I was done, I wasn't going to put myself through this level of pain and discomfort to be used by vindictive curtain twitchers. I put my pen down, switched off my computer and walked over to the Inspectors office,

"I'm done boss, I can't take this pain anymore, I have to go sick"

I hobbled back to my car, sat sideways in my seat and dragged my legs into the car one by one, I knew at that point I was finished in the Police. I had 7 years left to do for a full pension at 55 years old, I doubted that I would ever be medically fit for service again. The 'job' had taken enough from me over the past 22 years, my marriage, my health, and at times my sanity. I had left the world of Covert Policing behind some years before and in an attempt at family life; I settled down to 'normal' work, although there is never a 'normal' day in front line Police work, I was promoted to Sergeant and began to enjoy the life of a team leader who was ready to support his officers and build a strong team. However, my career was now gone, I was deemed not medically fit for service! My career had been robbed from me by football hooligans, I have never had much time for these types anyway, but now I hold them with a greater level of disdain.

Reading through this chapter of the book I wondered if I had begun to sound bitter and twisted about my situation and the way that the Police Service had changed over the past few years. Maybe I have earnt the right to feel a bit nauseated by the public and disappointed at our leaders, but if I do, it is only a fleeting feeling! I have had over 30 years' service to the Army and the Police and there are many other tales of my service that I may write about in the future. I made some big mistakes in the early years, but in general I've had the time of my life, I wouldn't change any of it. But for now I only wanted to share what I thought was the most interesting and rewarding parts of my life and Police Career. There is no feeling I can compare to the adrenalin rush of an undercover drugs buy, or that burning sensation in your chest after a footchase with a criminal, it's a drug in itself, and like most drugs its addictive.

The war on drugs will continue to be fought on the streets of the UK and around the world, my thoughts on it that are; Until we realise that prohibition is pointless, there will always be criminals making a lot of money from the trade. Drugs are too engrained in society for them to just disappear overnight, we could have bombed and burnt the poppy fields of Afghanistan to eradicate Heroin, but our governments chose not to, why is that? Perhaps my theory about drug addiction funding economies is not too far from the truth; no drugs mean's no addicts, no addict's equal's low crime rates, and the need for the whole justice system grinds to a halt! That means a lot of jobs, legal aid and health care that attracts millions of pounds and dollars in government contracts, and we know who gets those don't we, that's right, friends of the political elites!

Anyway, I had now paid my final debt to society; The public had had their monies worth from me, and now broken, I am to be thrown out like a broken piece of equipment, and to be honest, I am happy with that decision. I have never been under the illusion that I am nothing more than a number, a replaceable cog in a bigger machine which will grind on without me.

It is now time for me to put myself first and live the best life that I could, I now have the time to plan my next adventures…

This book is printed on paper from sustainable sources managed under the Forest Stewardship Council (FSC) scheme.

It has been printed in the UK to reduce transportation miles and their impact upon the environment.

For every new title that Matador publishes, we plant a tree to offset CO_2, partnering with the More Trees scheme.

MORE TREES
LET'S PLANT A BILLION TREES

For more about how Matador offsets its environmental impact, see www.troubador.co.uk/about/